ND COMES • U...

I'LL BE THE

POSITION OF THESE

OUT AN END THERE

ING • SO I WILL

H ON TO VICTORY •

E ME • THE FIRE

MARCH ON TO

MY FEET BLEED

BRAND BY HAND

JON CONTINO

Editor: John Gall with Alicia Tan
Designer: Jon Contino
Production Manager: Rebecca Westall

Library of Congress Control Number: 2017956789

ISBN: 978-1-4197-3224-9
eISBN: 978-1-68335-317-1

Printed and bound in China
10 9 8 7 6 5 4 3 2 1

BLISTERS, CALLUSES, and CLIENTS: A LIFE IN DESIGN

Jon Contino

ABRAMS, NEW YORK

FOREWORD........10
FAMILY..........16
NEW YORK......24
AMERICANA.......54
BASEBALL........76
MARITIME......108
SECRET SOCIETY......120
TATTOO..........128
AFTER DARK.....146
HARDCORE.....164
HORROR.......178
FEAR........190
VICES.......220
ACKNOWLEDGMENTS.....238

FOR

ERIN & FIONA

MY REASON
FOR BEING

POCKET SKETCHBOOK

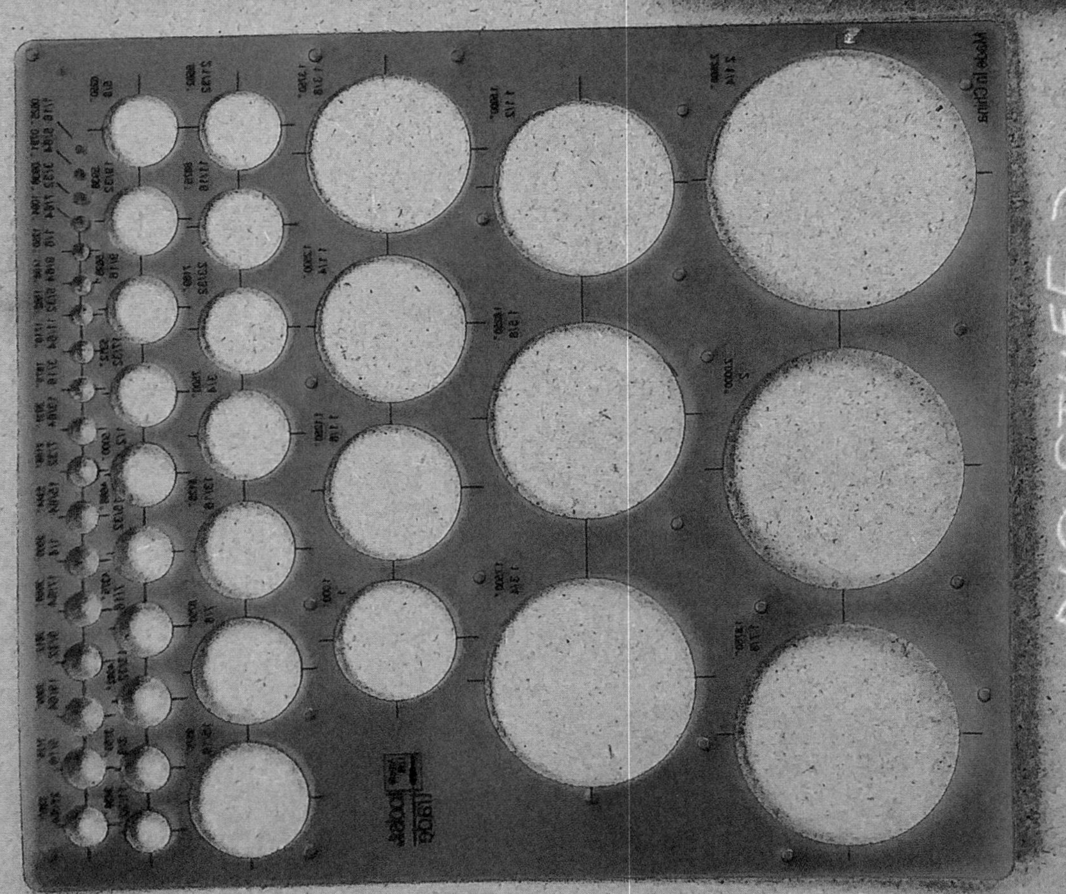

IPAD

APPLE PENCIL

FOREWORD BY TODD RADOM

Jon Contino is a time traveler. His work seems to come to us from some undefined, distant age, an era when people worked with their hands and skillfully created things of real and lasting value. The maker's own hand is there, and the work is purposeful and expressive, an elegant synthesis of both form and function.

For some time now, the word "artisan" has been thrown around with reckless abandon. It's become a debased term that has been stripped of any significance or real meaning. There is artisanal fast food, for instance, and there is bespoke software. Seriously. Jon Contino, however, is the real deal. He is a master craftsman and an artist whose work overflows with personality and authenticity.

Jon is one of those rare designers who has been able to tame technology and bend it to his will. Many if not most designers think digitally first, a case of the tail wagging the dog. Jon's skilled hand is his greatest weapon, and his process, while not unique, represents a commitment to craft that contains few shortcuts or digital bells and whistles. Every line, every blip and divot, and each and every seemingly random detail has been sweated over and judiciously employed to maximum effect. He makes it all look so effortless, but there's tension in his work that belies the obvious.

Jon's work is full of paradoxes, contrasts, and contradictions. Exquisitely graceful letterforms reside side by side with multitudes of skulls and crossbones, grim reapers, coffins, rats, snakes, and sewer-dwelling alligators.

At first glance, his work can seem chaotic, chock-full of swooping angles, dramatic flourishes, and seemingly disparate pieces that somehow join together in harmonious fashion. And yet there is order within all of this tumult. All of this wonderfully resolved chaos seems like the perfect visual metaphor for New York, the artist's hometown. Jon's hand and his mind are indisputably a product of where he is from, and that dynamic drives him and defines his work.

Jon Contino is a New Yorker. He looks and sounds like a New Yorker. His ever-present Yankees cap announces him as a New Yorker, just in case the rest of him somehow gives pause. Like Jon, I am a native, born and educated on the island of Manhattan. A couple of decades separate us, but we share the influences, cadence, and rhythm of our home region.

Los Angeles now claims to be "the creative capital of the world," Miami's art scene is energetic and vibrant, and there are those who say that the West Coast is the new Madison Avenue. Some of these things may well be true, but the fact is that New York remains the most competitive place on earth for us creative professionals, a place that has been known to swallow lesser people whole. Like me, Jon embraces both the challenges and the rewards that come with living and working in our field, in our area, and the absolute need to prove ourselves every single day.

Jon Contino is tireless. I've told him that he needs a vacation, but he refuses to listen. He is prolific. He is everywhere. He is a magician.

Here in the second half of the second decade of the third millennium, Jon may well be the most imitated designer out there—and yes, "imitated" can also serve as a veiled euphemism for "ripped off." His perfectly imperfect style has inspired a sea of pretenders, but make no mistake, nobody can pull off this look like Jon can. For my money, it's all about his skillful use of composition and negative space. Jon's work is balanced and harmonious, with each and every element masterfully deployed in service to the whole.

Jon Contino is a perfectionist. Skills aside, all of that balled-up New York angst propels his art to an elevated place. He massages the minutiae within his work and cares about stuff that few of us would recognize as anything less than what's ultimately a perfect realization.

Jon Contino is a throwback. There was a time when graphic design really was a cut-and-paste profession, a vocation where hand skills were both necessary and valuable. I cut my teeth in publishing and advertising doing hand-lettering in the 1980s, back in the days before digitization made lettering accessible, understandable, and approachable to the masses. I look at Jon's letterforms and think back to those days, imagining him, like me back then, making it all happen with pen and ink, razor blades, drafting tools, and rubber cement.

Finally, Jon is also a devoted family man, a generous friend, and an artist whose work I admire and respect. He is smart, eloquent, and witty, and his art is defined by those attributes just as much as his technique and style. The man, like his work, is both honest and earnest, overflowing with New York attitude. In an age where visual impressions are abundant yet fleeting, Jon Contino's work stands out as the definitive design look of our time, delivered from a faraway era, built by hand.

Todd Radom
December 2017

SEPT.
PERFOR
ISLE OF MAN
19 07
RIDE OR DIE
BY ANY MEANS NECESSARY
Lo's Angeles, Calif.
540 S. SANTE FE AVE.
ESTD 1990
LUCKY BRAND C
HE WHO KEEPS HIS TONGUE KEEPS HIS TONGUE. KEEPS HIS FRIENDS! KEEPS
"V" FOR VICTORY
U.S.
ARAGON
ESTEBAN BAGLIETTO
ALFREDO SCARPATTI
SANTIAGO SANA
JUAN & TEODORO FARENGA
REPUBLICA DEL LA BOCA 1905
CRAFTMANSHIP
INSPIRATION
EXECUTION
etc.
HOME IS YOUR HEART
Industrial
MILITARY
Jon Contino
NEW YORK U.S.A.
W O R K
THE DRUNKEN BOTANIST
THE PLANTS THAT CREATE THE WORLD'S GREAT DRINKS
"EVERY GREAT DRINK STARTS WITH A PLANT"
AMY STEWART
AUTHOR OF WICKED PLANTS
A NEW YORK TIMES BESTSELLER
ALGONQUIN BOOKS OF CHAPEL HILL
DRUNKEN BOTANIST STEWART
JOURNAL STANDARD FURNITURE
MILITARY
TRAD
Work
WORK
Trad MILITARY
U.S.A.
New York, N.Y.
RUN HUNGRY TASTE VICTORY
VCXC
GREATNESS STARTS HERE BRONX, N.Y.
CEMETERY HILL
BRONX
BRONX-NY-NYC

18×24
WITH
SPECIAL
LIVE!
PERFORMING AT N
9/30
St. Louis
MISSOURI
AT
New York
DON'T TREAD ON ME
DIVE
PEACE
ALL AMERICAN
Watch it
NEW YORK
DEAD END
UNION
QUALITY GOODS
JOIN OR DIE
27
BASEBALL CLUB
47
56
Royals
SEALS BASEBALL
M 51 BA
51
BASEBALL CLUB
MINNEAPOLIS MILLERS
CHICAGO B.B.CLUB
OAKLAND B.B. CLUB
BASE-BALL CLUB
44
FEDS
118
SEATTLE BALL CLUB
55
BROOKLYN
B.B.B.C.C.
The
MYSTIC ORDER
OF THE DEEP
SHELLBACK
CARIBBEAN
SPICED RUM
Vintage Clothing
New!
EXTINCTION AD
FOR REAL
FOR M
BY MAX

Family

I REMEMBER WHEN I WAS A KID, MY EYES WERE ALWAYS SURVEYING THE ENVIRONMENT AROUND ME.

They would wander around the room, glance across the TV screen, or scan book spines lining a shelf. Just like any impressionable youth, I was constantly soaking up the world. Maybe I did it slightly differently, though. You see, I spent the majority of my childhood drawing and drawing and drawing, but unlike other kids, I wasn't sitting there drawing fire trucks and boring-ass superheroes. I was studying the composition and linework of the *Ghostbusters* logomark and perfecting the interlocking N-Y monogram from my Yankees baseball hat. This is how I spent my time, and my family noticed.

My family is made up of creative people, and I didn't realize when I was younger, but kids absorb everything they see, and all that information shapes their brains and the way they interact with the world.

My father was a carpenter. I watched him make something out of nothing time and time again—analyzing space, making a plan, and constructing the previously unconstructed all with his own two hands. He's also the first person I ever knew who was his own boss. Making your own schedule in a way that allowed you to be the most productive is essentially what I learned "work" to be. It took me a few years before I figured out most people don't live that way. And on top of all this, my father always had a charming way of explaining the rules of the world. Spouting hilarious one-liners and stories of past experiences, he basically taught me how to be a human bullshit detector. Every anecdote always ended with a moral of sorts—about why it's important to think before you act, and why the people who don't are assholes.

My mother, on the other hand, was more of a fine artist. She would draw everything from architecturally accurate building renders, to beautifully scripted calligraphic invitations, to watercolor landscapes and fashion illustrations. Her ability to re-create an image on a page was flawless. And she did it with such ease and elegance that it cemented into my head the idea that anything was possible with pen and paper. Her natural talents illuminated my young mind and seemed to be handed down to me by some sort of osmosis. She made drawing look so easy that it never really felt like something I wouldn't be able to do.

Then I had my grandparents.

My grandfather was an engineer who had worked with companies like AT&T and Bell Labs on the biggest monstrosities the world has ever seen. (We call them "computers.") Legend has it he even worked on one of the teams that developed UNIX, the operating system that eventually led to the development of macOS, the very same operating system I'm using to write these words. On any given day, he would show up at our house with a science kit or some electronic device he wanted to show me how to build. Circuits and miniature light bulbs lit up a good portion of my childhood. And these mini engineering lessons also came with a dose of my grandfather's dry wit. An intellectual joke that most people wouldn't get, or didn't want to get, was his specialty. And he was famous for it. To this very day, I often smile when I think about how my grandfather would catch a tongue-in-cheek reference I'd made in a campaign, or a tagline with a double meaning I sold to a client. Something to make people think or laugh, or even better, both.

And last, but certainly not least, was my grandmother. Everyone knew her and everyone loved her. She used to tell me about how she would cut class and head over to Ebbets Field to catch a Dodgers game or how she used to play stickball with the boys on her block and beat them on the field, and with her words. She was not a quiet person. She was loud and hilarious and spoke her mind, but she was also thoughtful. She constantly went out of her way to help others. Family, friends, strangers—it didn't matter. Her heart was the biggest part of her already massive personality. But besides that, she was enamored with the arts and she nurtured the hell out of my own obsession during the many days we spent together, taking the role of Backup Mom while my parents dealt with the challenges of caring for my brother. During those days, she would take me to Pearl Paint and literally buy me anything I wanted. Pencils, pens, markers, notebooks, pads, how-to books on cartooning and illustration. She fed my creative habits and she pushed me day after day to keep trying new things. She always made it feel like we were learning together, too, even though she clearly knew what was going on.

Oh, and I almost forgot to mention the great-grandparents and countless cousins, aunts, and uncles who all had some hand in the arts. The creative gene was clearly a dominant one in my family.

chris '76

The Mary Louis Academy
Art Department
Catalog for 1973-74

Between my mother, father, and grandmother, there was always someone doing something creative in my house. Designing, sketching, building, decorating—there was no shortage of interesting handiwork for me to watch. One time in particular, I remember my mother being commissioned by our church to render the building for the masthead of the weekly newsletter. She was well aware of my interest in art at this point, so she brought me along for all of her drawing sessions.

She set up shop in the King Kullen supermarket parking lot across the street from the church to get the perfect three-quarter angle. I sat in the front seat of the car with my mother while she got out all her supplies and began furiously sketching and refining before traffic got too busy to see what was going on. Witnessing the process of laying out a composition, building it, and refining it was a great lesson at the time and something I clearly do a lot of these days.

Angie

E · PLURIB
UNUM
V. Busci

E Pluribus Unum

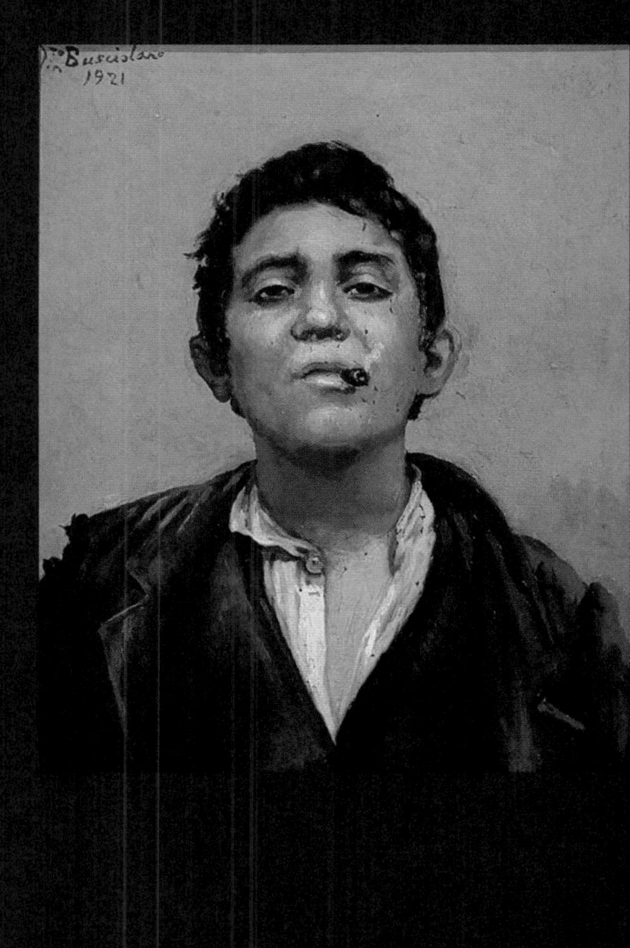
1921

NEW
YORK

Being from New York and coming from a family chasing after the American Dream has always been a major source of pride for me.

Ours is a story like many other families'. In the early 1900s, ancestors on both sides of my family came over to Ellis Island from southern Italy and settled in the lower part of Manhattan, which, of course, became known as Little Italy. Slowly they moved out to Brooklyn, then Queens, and finally Long Island. As a third-generation Italian American with roots in the heart of New York, I've looked at the city as another piece of the family tree. The love for this place boils over in my blood. I can't help myself, it feels like it's part of my soul. And you can see it and hear it in the rest of my family, too. It seems that all of our stories involve the city streets themselves as a vital character.

My family's story, and those of so many families like mine, make up the fabric that is New York. So many different cultures and beliefs all crammed into a tight little space sitting right on the Atlantic Ocean. The charisma radiates from New Yorkers, because even though we've all become Americans, there are threads of everyone's original culture that can't help but shine through. It's part of what makes this place great. To be a New Yorker means you can identify with an old history while simultaneously building a new one. A style is born out of this contradiction. The influences of the old meet the challenges of the new. The way homes are decorated for the holidays, with both traditional motifs and sparkly new gadgetry, always struck me as a great example of this idea. People take what they know and enhance it to demonstrate their ability to evolve. On the street, you might hear a hundred different languages, but walk long enough and the strange words you've heard eventually get lifted and blended into New Yorkese. A language you can understand. These fusions of culture contribute to the creative fabric of New York, appearing in music, graffiti, dance, and other art forms. There is a never-ending source of brilliance around every corner.

As a kid growing up in Long Island, I was a train ride away from the greatest city in the world. It meant a lot to have the city looming over my head in my developmental years. Every opportunity in the world was right outside my front door. I admired the graffiti-covered train cars and buildings next to billboards from multimillion-dollar ad campaigns. The juxtaposition was not lost on me, even as a young kid.

Even walking the streets looking for trouble always led to finding the most interesting places. One time in high school a few friends and I went down to St. Mark's Place because someone heard you could pick up a really legit-looking fake ID from some shady guy with a souped-up photocopier or something. I never fooled around with controlled substances so it didn't really matter to me, but I loved the exploratory aspect of these trips, so I tagged along whenever I could. I remember walking into this dumpy little storefront with my friends, who were getting psyched for the possibilities a fake ID held, but what I noticed was a poorly lit room full of giant printers, garbage computers, and a ton of weird art equipment piled on top of tables. I was blown away. Something so meaningless was coming out of a real-deal art studio. I mean, that's what it was. There's no reason to call it anything but that. This guy was designing and producing in-house for a profit, and it really made me think of the possibilities. I had already been doing similar stuff for bands, and ironically enough, I was getting really good at forging stuff like graduation tickets and school IDs in my spare time, but this was a whole new level. This was a real business, it was interesting, and it clearly wasn't playing by anyone's rules.

Some people like to point to the bright lights and big names of New York as the peak of creativity, but I think that's all bullshit. For me, the true inspiration comes from the everyday people on the streets making a living—doing it the only way they know how. Being creative on a budget. Using the limited resources at their disposal and getting inventive with it. This is the New York I know and love and the reason I'm so eager to slap it on every little thing I do.

Project LOOP, 2013

Hand-painted skateboard

This piece signifies an evolution in style, one that I've described as "New York City Folk." Drawing influence from the characteristics of Asian, Central American, and Egyptian folk art, the style removes volume and realism and focuses on flat, iconic imagery with a more geometric approach to organic forms. With that as a foundation, I used New York City–centric objects, creatures, and motifs like subway mosaics and graffiti to develop a visual language that juxtaposes Manhattan's modern tone with its natural rawness and grime.

N.Y.C.
AGAINST ALL ADVERSITY
NEVER FALTER

GOOD FOR ONE FARE
NYC

Adidas x Parley, 2016
Triptych design artist series

Labels designed for water bottles to be sold in the Adidas NYC flagship store

ABOVE:
UFC, 2017
Fight Night Long Island

Logos for UFC Fight Night at Nassau Coliseum, five minutes from where I grew up. How could I say no?

OPPOSITE TOP:
Nike, 2012
Nike Football Society

OPPOSITE BOTTOM:
New Balance, 2012
Run NYC

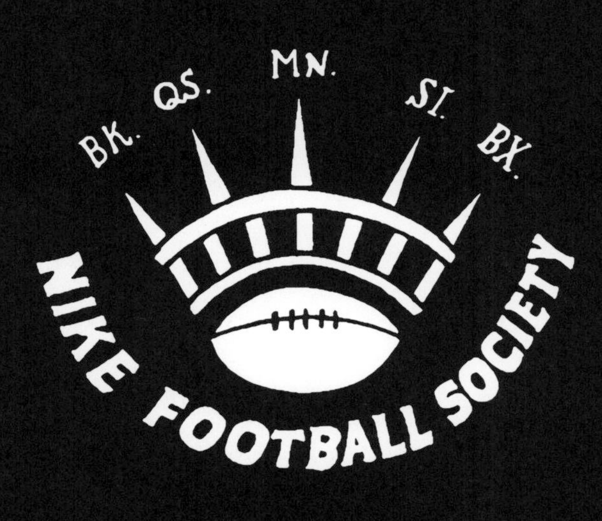

RUN!
BRONX
BROOKLYN
MANHATTAN
QUEENS
STATEN ISLAND
2012

Green Fingers Market, 2016

This collage of icons was designed as a promotional image and for an in-store mural to celebrate the three-year anniversary of Green Fingers Market, a shop in Manhattan's Lower East Side that's part plant nursery, part lifestyle boutique.

Nº5
RIVINGTON
NEW YORK
N.Y.
G.F.
20
02
Green
Fingers
20
02
NYC★TYO
GREEN
OR
DIE
Lower
East
Side
GROW
Nº5
RIVINGTON
NEW YORK
N.Y.
G.F.
GREEN
OR
DIE
Lower
GROW
DAMN IT
Lower
East
Side
GF

NEW YORK
RAISED ME

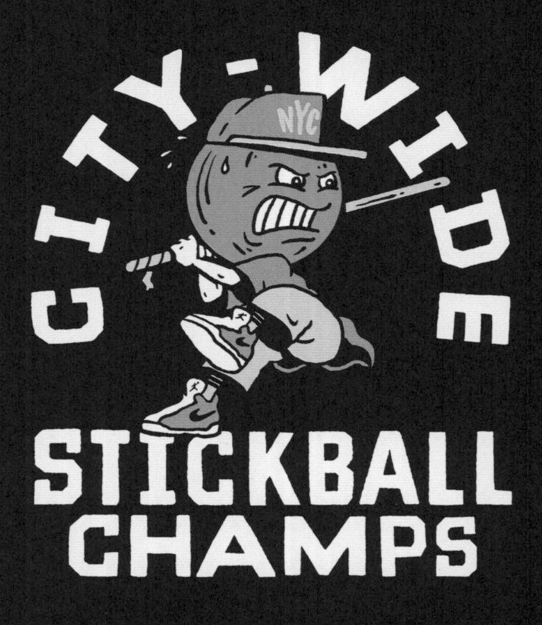

OPPOSITE:

Nike SoHo, 2017

Artist customization collection

Customers selected designs to be printed on a clothing item of their choice.

ABOVE:

Nike SoHo, 2017

Laser-etched Air Force 1 sneakers

ABOVE:
Nike SoHo, 2017
Artist customization collection

OPPOSITE:
Nike SoHo, 2017
Hand-painted canvas, approximately five feet tall, that hung in the retail space

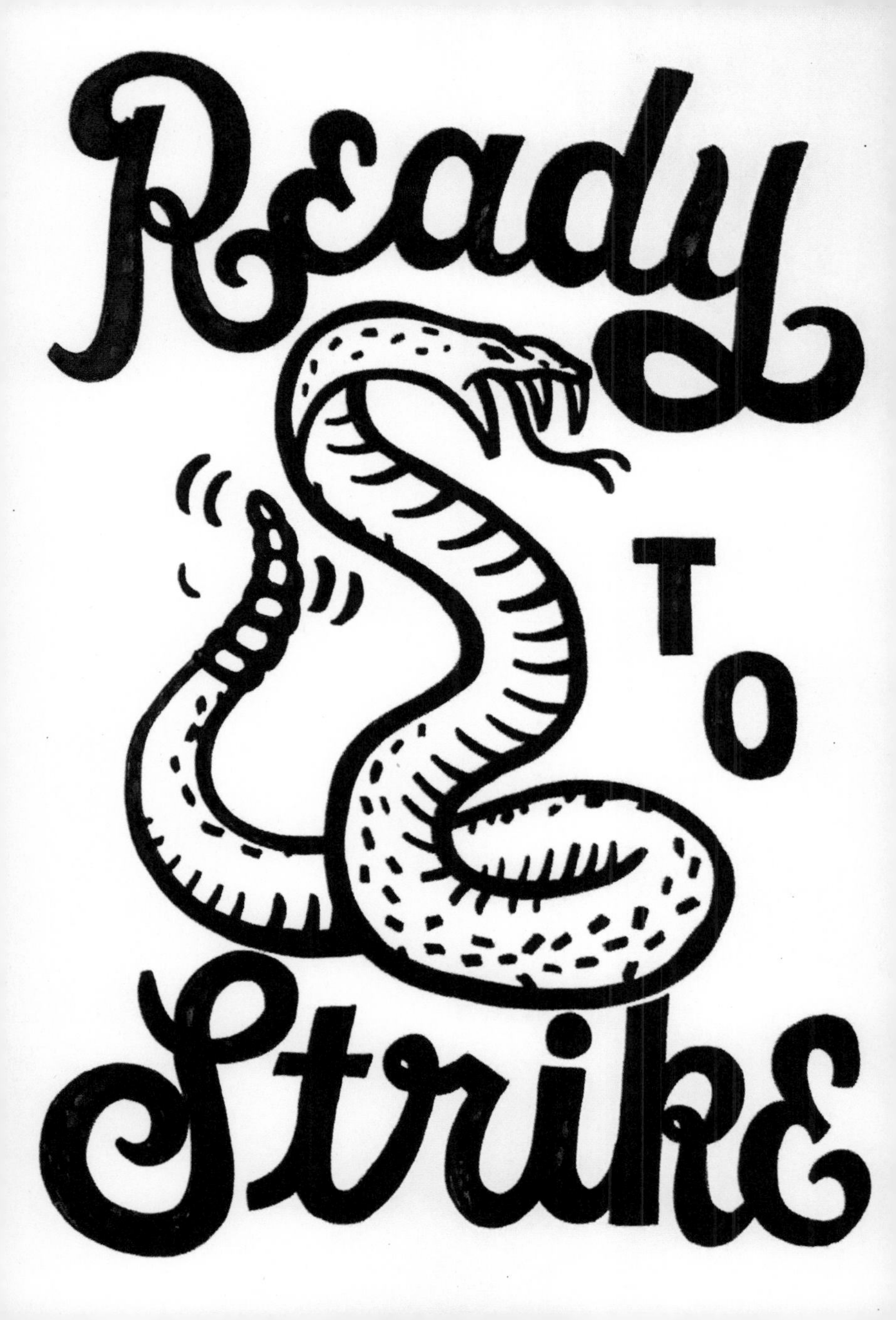
Ready
To
Strike

217
NYC
UFC
Fight for Yours
NY
217
NY
UFC
Respect the Fight
Own the Night
Keep It Clean
with Honor
with Pride
New York City
No Place to Hide
217
Fight
Grade
Ultimate
N.Y.C.
UFC 217
Honor · Respect · Strength · Discipline ·
217
NYC

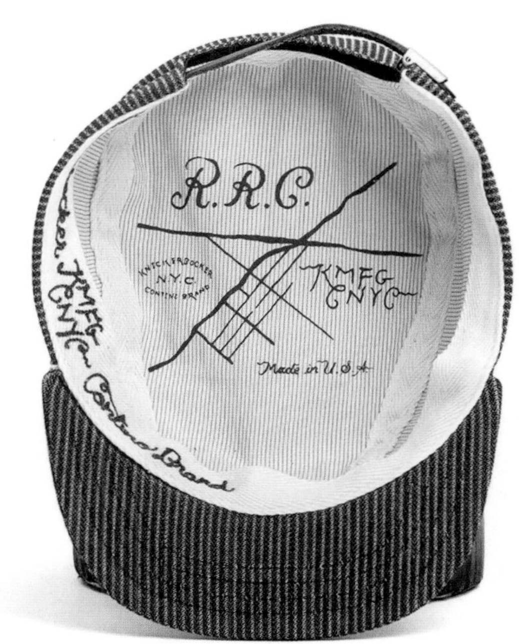

ABOVE:

Knickerbocker Mfg. Co., 2014

Collaboration with New York–based hat and menswear manufacturer. The illustrated maps inside the hats show the location of the Knickerbocker shop, near the Ridgewood Reservoir, the body of water that happens to connect the neighborhood of the shop and the neighborhood where I grew up. Who knew?

OPPOSITE:

UFC, 2017

Branding and icon design for the "UFC 217" event at Madison Square Garden in NYC. All participants wore apparel with these illustrations during the week leading up to and on the night of the event.

ABOVE:

Brooklyn Nets, 2012

Mock rebrand commissioned by art and design blog *The Fox Is Black* for an article critiquing the Brooklyn Nets' new identity

OPPOSITE, CLOCKWISE FROM TOP LEFT:

H&M, 2013; Silk Road Cycles, 2010; Kiehl's, 2013, mural design for the first Kiehl's flagship store outside of Manhattan, in Brooklyn Heights

Thieves of N.Y.

SILK ROAD CYCLES

JON CON

JCNYC, 2016
Poster print

The JCNYC brand encompasses everything I do that is not client work. It is a creative and emotional outlet as well as a place to experiment. And in typical Jon Contino fashion, it's a place for me to turn my ideas into something I can make and sell.

CXXVI CLOTHING Co. of NEW YORK

CXXVI was an exercise in patience. It was a constantly evolving monstrosity with a mind of its own. Matt Gorton and I started the brand after receiving a cease and desist from Disney for making and selling bootleg *Lost* T-shirts. Our plan had been pretty brilliant. Make "cool" T-shirts for people who love *Lost*, sell them online, make a bunch of cash, and then have money to buy Christmas presents for our families. It worked really well until that letter came in the mail. Then we stopped because we didn't want to go to jail.

At this point in time, the economy was getting flushed down the toilet and our graphic design studio had just lost our two biggest clients—the ones who were essentially paying to make sure we could live. It seemed like everything we did was born out of a need to survive, so it's no wonder the clothing company started, and ended, the way it did.

To make a long story short (and it is a long story), Matt and I used our poor-man ingenuity to make the brand seem like something when it was actually nothing. We printed the shirts in our studio, Matt photographed them, I built the website, and then we proceeded to pretend like we were some hotshot company that was selling one-of-a-kind, high-end items with handcrafted details and trim. In our head, this was a great scheme. Our printing was shoddy, all of our equipment ended up breaking or melting down, and there were endless amounts of malfunctions, rips, tears, stains, and fury to follow. But somehow we made it work. We turned the flaws into the charm of the brand.

But eventually, the universe turned on us. A bad business deal beat us into the ground and Hurricane Sandy finished us off, leaving us with financial troubles and very little of our studio, inventory, and brand. Our friendship was nearly destroyed because of this, but just as the brand restarted, so did our lives. We kept marching forward and didn't let it break our spirits.

We had started the brand out of desperation. Just a couple of hardcore kids making something the only way we knew how. Within a short amount of time people started to give a shit about what we were doing. CXXVI hit the market at just the right time. It was different, it was raw, and it came from people who had no idea what the hell they were doing. The brand struck a chord, and we finally found a voice for ourselves and learned who we were as human beings and designers.

"The Hardcore Logo," 2009

This logo was a good opportunity to make use of a big *X* and was designed as a reference to our roots.

"The Nautical Logo," 2010

Nautical was everything to CXXVI, so we made sure people knew it at all times.

"The Handcrafted Logo," 2011

We embraced the hands-on nature of the brand and started pushing it in every aspect.

"The Surly Logo," 2012

This is the "we've had enough of this shit" logo, and it rode into the sunset with us.

OUR ANCHORS
WE WILL
weigh
OUR SAILS
WE
WILL
SET
the
FRIENDS
N.Y.
WE ARE
LEAVING
we
will
NEVER
FORGET.

ABOVE:
Some of the most iconic CXXVI illustrations were imitated by companies large and small. I've even ripped myself off. For example, the "Cape Horn" whale concept became the basis of the identity for the Hidden Sea, a wine-brand client I worked with from 2011 to 2017 (see pages 224–225).

OPPOSITE:
The trim work for CXXVI helped put the brand on the map. Every hangtag, label, and package was printed, dyed, or made by hand, and they became collectors' items for our customers. That was never the intention, but it was a pleasant surprise when people started sharing photos of their tag collections with us.

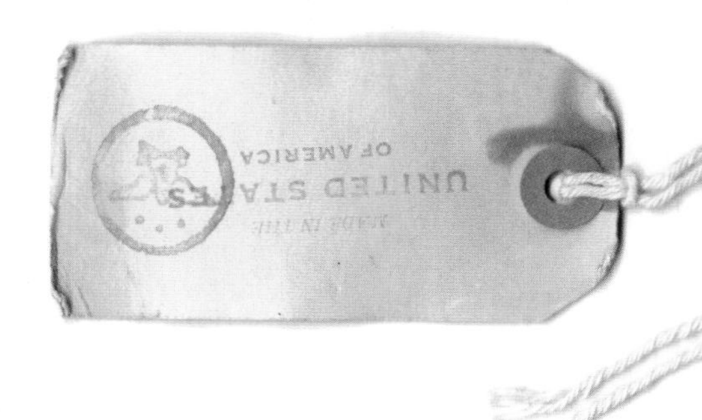

CXXVI CLOTHING Co
NEW YORK, N.Y.
MADE IN U.S.A.
MANUFACTURED: JUL 20 2011

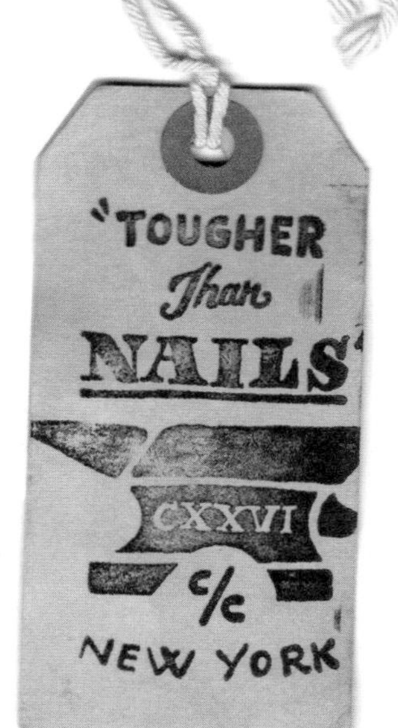

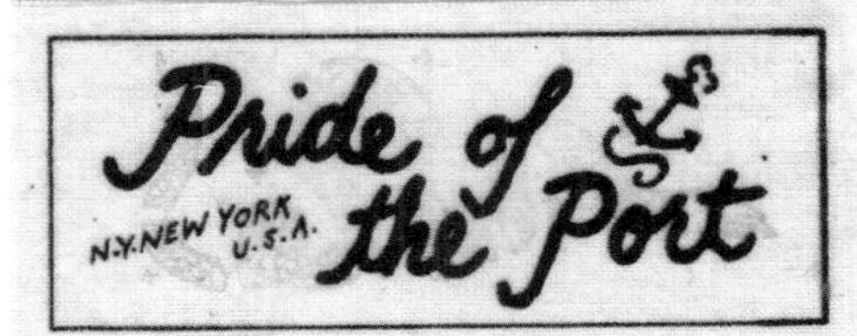

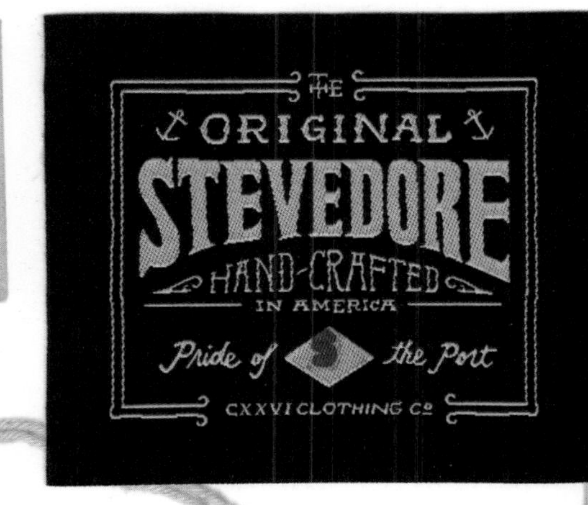

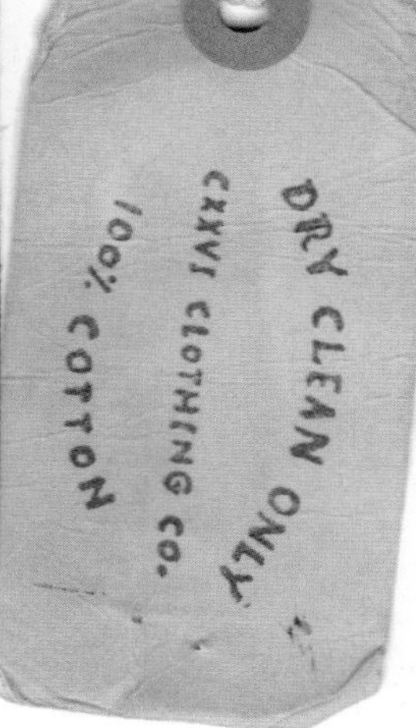

LIBE

DEA

"Liberty or Death" organically became the mantra of CXXVI. This particular lettering was a quick, one-off sketch that ended up as a core element of the ever-growing visual identity. The shortening of the historical phrase, the rough pencils, and the lack of finesse communicates everything the brand came to represent.

CXXVI had an endless number of illustrations with a focus on all things nautical, New York, blue-collar, and troublemaking.

MADE BY PROJECT
CXXVI
CLOTHING CO.
T-SHIRTS $35
HAND-DYED BANDANAS $25
PRINTED TOTE $30
HAND-DRAWN TOTE $65
ENGRAVED ZIPPO $75
14"x17" PRINTS $25
ANCHOR NECKLACE $55
MONKEY FIST $15
CASH! CREDIT!
"A Gentleman's Brand"
SEAL of QUALITY
NEW YORK
U.S.A.
GENUINE
HAND-MADE
MENSWEAR
CXXVI CLOTHING CO.
NEW YORK, N.Y.
UNITED STATES

TOUGHER
Than
NAILS'
c/c
NEW YORK

CXXVI CLOTHING Co
OF
NEW YORK
C.C.N.Y.
100% HIGH QUALITY
AMERICAN
MADE
"T" SHIRT
PRODUCT LINE
C/C
REG.
TRADE
MARK
U.S.A.
MEDIUM
MACHINE WASH COLD. TUMBLE DRY LOW
DO NOT BLEACH!

AMERICANA

The History of the United States has always intrigued me.

Sure, the country is big and powerful and corrupt as ever in the twenty-first century, but you can never take away its humble yet brave beginnings. I've always been a fan of the underdog. Maybe because I was a small kid who felt like he always had something to prove. Hell, who am I kidding. I'm still trying to prove myself to this day. And America was for a long time an underdog, too. Knowing that a bunch of colonial troublemakers took on the world's biggest army and won is something that's always resonated with me. Dedication, passion, and a relentless spirit can conquer any obstacles.

The country's identity as the "Land of Opportunity" and how that identity has been represented over the years is an endless source of inspiration. From the first handwoven, unofficial flags to the delicate details carved into each and every monument, this nation is an aesthetic gold mine. It's bold and it's fearless. At its core, it has a purity you won't find anywhere else. It's traditional and modern all in the same breath, because there's no rule book to tell us otherwise. Essentially, we started from nothing, cobbled together a foundation from our various backgrounds, and continue to develop our motley culture to this day.

The iconography associated with this history includes some seriously striking imagery: soaring bald eagles and bold stars and stripes, primary colors that can't be mistaken, a fiery torch held aloft in the night sky by a towering statue.

There is nothing delicate about all this. This is raw and brutal and filled with passion. This imagery represents determination and strength in the face of adversity. Aesthetically speaking, it all remains relatively simple. The best message is the one you can communicate in the least amount of lines.

But besides all that beautiful and direct patriotic iconography, there are other cultural touchstones I draw on.

One not-so-obvious one is the newspaper. The *New York Times*, the *Washington Post* . . . these are icons unto themselves, born out of an instinctual desire to disseminate information. Then there's my beloved baseball, played by a group of people who once called themselves a "club." Legend has it the sport was developed right here in my home state of New York (the myth was debunked, but . . . that's not the point). And then there's mom-and-pop stores. With those, you know what you're getting: a friendly neighborhood face with a determination to grab your attention. (But you know what, we all pay attention to them even if their storefronts are terribly designed.) Crooked letters, mismanaged font styles, poor color choices, and questionable illustrations can still keep your attention just as long as, if not longer than, polished works of brand design.

Newspapers, baseball teams, mom-and-pop stores. All of these things share a sort of DIY attitude of starting from scratch and doing things their own way to accomplish their goals. Mix all this stuff up into one bag and you've got yourself a genuine aesthetic we call Americana. A combination of rebellious spirit, tough-as-nails work ethic, and an insatiable desire to prove something is what creates an honest and inspiring frame of reference.

Swimsuit 2015

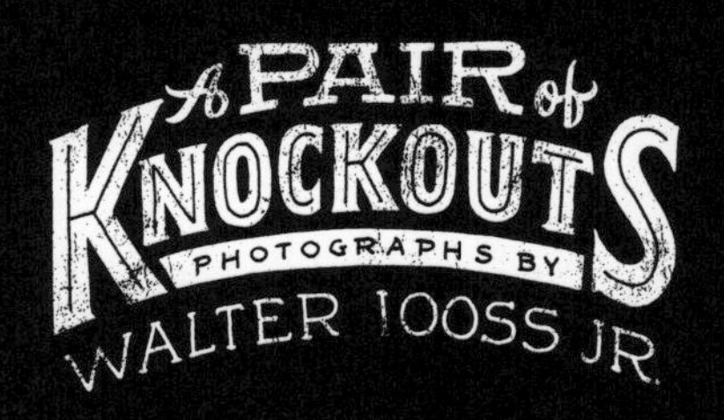

A PAIR of
KNOCKOUTS
PHOTOGRAPHS BY
WALTER IOOSS JR.

Rookies

Hay, Now
Photographs by BEN WATTS

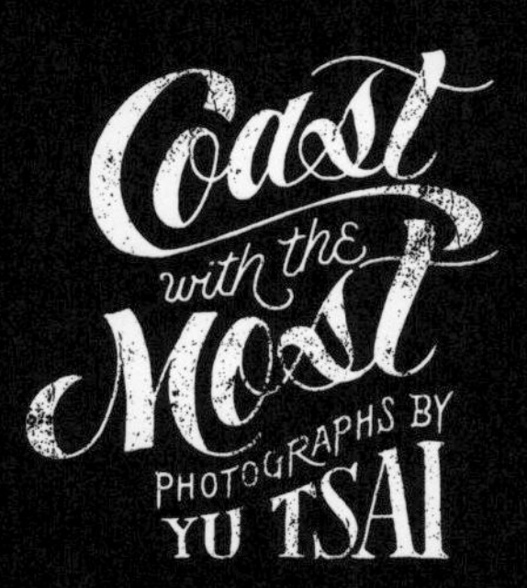

Sports Illustrated, 2015

Swimsuit issue logotype branding and design

BLKSMTH
80 NASSAU AVE BROOKLYN, N.Y.

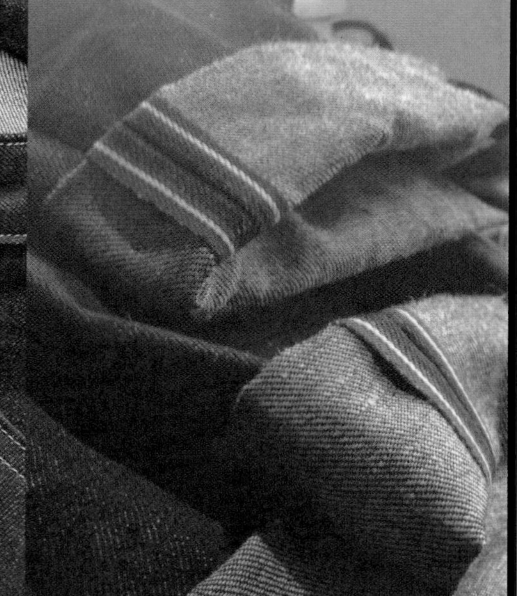

UNDER 2 FLAGS

U.T.F. Mfg. Co.

U.K. N.Y.

OPPOSITE:

BLKSMTH, 2011

Identity and trim package

ABOVE:

Under Two Flags, 2011

"Saville Row to the LES" T-shirt collection

C&M
MFG.
U.S. REG.
TRADE-
MARK

Matix, 2012

USA Signature Collection

The tone of this collection ranged from surly to tongue-in-cheek.

"What doesn't break me will make me."

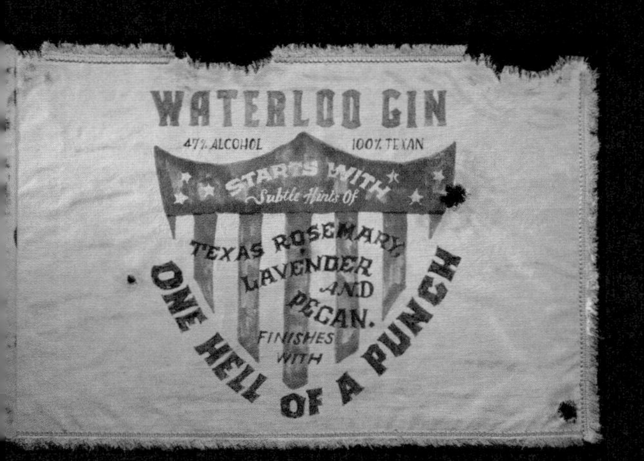

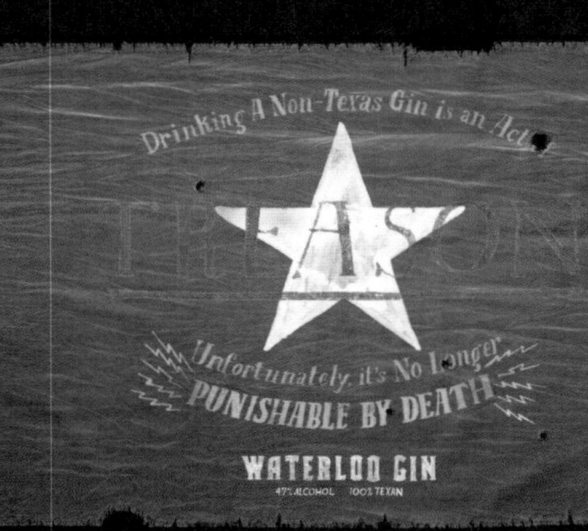

Waterloo Gin, 2011
Heritage flag designs

You want to talk authentic? These flags were shot with real guns to produce real bullet holes—Texas and Photoshop don't mix.

Hamilton Wood Type & Printing Museum, 2012,
"Flying U"

Home of the Brave, 2013
Restaurant branding

A little slice of America in Toronto, Canada

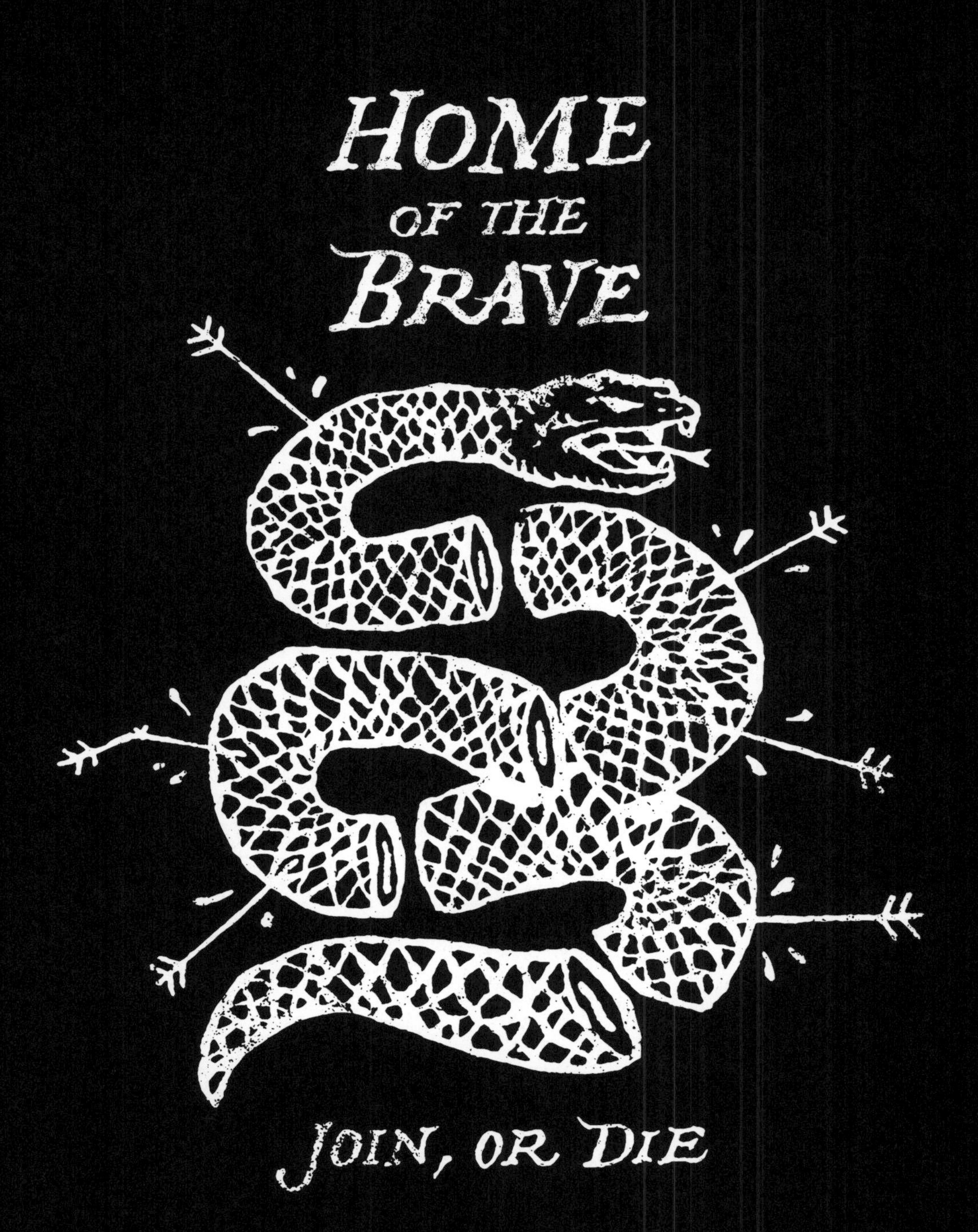
HOME
OF THE
BRAVE
JOIN, OR DIE

ABOVE FROM LEFT: The National, 2010, concert poster; The Soundtrack of America, 2016, festival poster

OPPOSITE: Newport Folk Festival, 2016, festival poster

NEWPORT
FOLK FESTIVAL™

Fort Adams State Park

2016

NEWPORT, R.I.

WOODEN
SLEEPERS

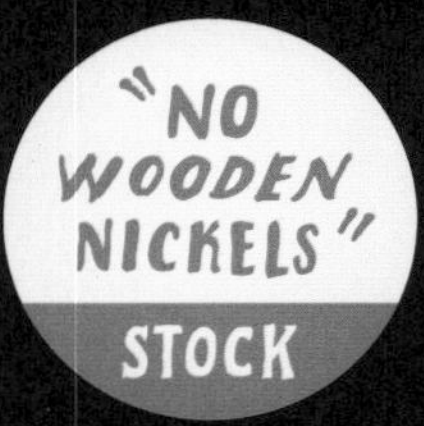
"NO
WOODEN
NICKELS"
STOCK

All Signs Point To
8
DEATH

MADE IN AMERICA
STOCK
MANUFACTURING
FINEST QUALITY

Live
Fast

NO
TO
EVERY
THING

STOCK
Mfg.

OVER
30
YEARS!

IMMOVABLE
E
IDEALS

JON
CONTINO
N.Y.

RESPECT

Stock
LEVEE
The

EVOLVE
U.S.A.

DEDICATED
To
PERFECTION

RED
W
S
HOOK

MY
WAY

ALL
NIGHTER

EVOLVE

C

WOODEN
SLEEPERS
RED HOOK
B'KLYN

Premium
& Precise

THINK
for
YOUR
SELF

STOCK
the
LEVEE

N
Y
C

INN
STOCK

SEAL
OF
APPROVAL

VAN
416
BRUNT

INN
STOCK

EVOLVE
U.S.A.

LEVEE

RED
HOOK
US
NEW
YORK

STOCK
U
S

U.S.A.
N.
Y.

LUCKY
13

INN STOCK

HOO
CARES?

CHICAGO
STOCK
ILLINOIS

STRESSED

Dedicated
To
Perfection

WOODEN
US
SLEEPERS

DRY
STOCK
GOODS

EVOLVE
L R C

N
C
Y

CHICAGO
STOCK
MFG. CO.
ILLINOIS

NEW
YORK
U.S.A.

HURLEY
4TH
OF
JULY

HURLEY

Hurley, 2017
Fourth of July apparel collection, final designs and concept sketches

PREVIOUS SPREAD:
Various clients, 2010–2014
Vintage-inspired pin-back buttons—always a favorite canvas for quick one-liners and minimal yet memorable illustrations

ABOVE:

Cherokee, 2011

Apparel designs for the clothing brand's USA Collection

OPPOSITE:

Yankee Doodle Dandy's, 2011

Food truck branding

ALL AMERICAN CHICKEN TENDERS
YANKEE DOODLE DANDY'S
MADE IN N.Y.C.
NEW YORK'S OWN
THE BEST CHICKEN TENDERS YOU'LL EVER EAT!
@USAFOODTRUCK ★ YANKEEDOODLEDANDYS.COM
REFRESHMENTS
ANTIBIOTIC and HORMONE-FREE
and SALAD
Yankee Doodle Dandy's INC.
58-97 54TH ST.
NEW YORK, N.Y.
11378

ALL AMERICAN CHICKEN TENDERS
USA
@USAFOODTRUCK
YANKEE DOODLE DANDY'S
MADE IN N.Y.C.
LIFE, LIBERTY and the PURSUIT of CHICKEN
Yankee Doodle Dandy's INC.
58-97 54TH ST.
NEW YORK, N.Y.
11378
ALL AMERICAN CHICKEN TENDERS

SHORT
FUSE
U.
S.
A.

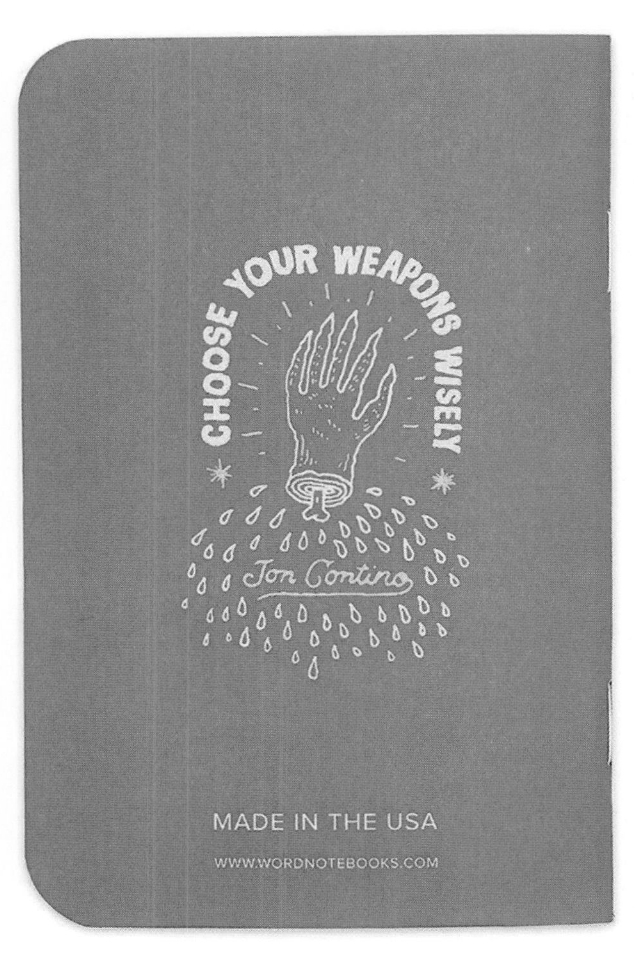

OPPOSITE:
Past Lives, 2016
Hand-painted enamel mugs

Past Lives is the brainchild of my wife, Erin Contino. The brand's primary focus is interior design, but it sells cool vintage finds as well. It's also an outlet for the two of us to collaborate on interesting and unique one-off projects.

ABOVE:
Word. Notebooks, 2016
Fourth of July special edition notebook, inspired by classic fireworks packaging

Baseball

I feel like I can distill everything in my life into three core concepts:

survival, tradition, and make-believe.

When I was not even two years old, my brother Nick was born with Down syndrome. This was the early 1980s, and it seemed like his diagnosis could only mean one thing: fear. Fear of the unknown, fear for the future, fear for health, fear for daily activities. He knocked on Death's door for the better part of two years. My parents were thrown a curveball they could've never expected. I spent days on end sitting in a hospital waiting room and sleeping in my grandparents' guest bedroom. But Nick was a fighter. He had no idea, but he was laughing in the face of doom and came out the other side victorious. Nick barely made it past his first breath, but thanks to some medical miracles and the instinct to survive, he's thriving and breakin' chops to this day, into his early thirties. But fear can sure do a number on a kid. Before I could even write my name, I understood Death was lurking. I knew at any moment a black drape could be pulled across an open window and that would be it.

That awareness, that fear will do funny things to you. You either take flight or you fight. And ever since my brother was born, all I did was fight. Eventually the fight in me morphed into aggression and a deadly competitive spirit. Suddenly I was fighting the world without even realizing it. Every obstacle in my way became a personal challenge as if the world was singling me out, betting on me to fail. Whether it was an actual physical fight with another person or something as simple as a portfolio review, I knew that my only option was to give it everything I had and not accept failure as an outcome. Survival, competition, failure, redemption. Life and death. It's all I've ever known.

Tradition has also been a part of me from the beginning—it's sewn into my family. We were Italian Americans living right outside the biggest, baddest city in the world and we weren't very long removed from "the boot." Sundays were "gravy" days, when my mother would spend most of the sun-drenched afternoon hovering over a stove speckled with tomato sauce and meat. On those days, a loaf of Italian bread wouldn't last long. As people passed through the kitchen, they would grab a piece of bread, dunk it in the gravy, and be on their way. Usually we'd find reasons to go back in the kitchen to get another dunk. I'm surprised there was anything left for dinner by the time my mother was done cooking.

Every last aunt, uncle, and cousin was always a few doors away. This always led to countless "drop-bys" from whoever was closest. There was never a dull moment in any of our homes. If people weren't stopping in to see us, we'd stop in to see someone else. And it wasn't just family either; this was a neighborhood thing, too. Ask any Italian how to handle seeing someone familiar while driving down the street, and they'll tell you: Stop the car in the middle of the street and talk about nothing important for the next forty-five minutes. If someone is trying to pass you, it's customary to get pissed off because they should know this conversation is of the utmost importance and requires the car to be sitting idle right in the middle of the street.

We grew up with an extremely social and emotional culture that doesn't question whether it's OK to yell at someone from across the street or give someone a smack to "knock some sense into them." The dinner table is a shouting match where no one ever wins. The kitchen is the heart of the home and host to hours upon hours of conversation, regardless of how uncomfortable it may be. As a kid, I soaked this all in and aspired to carry on the ways of my family. There was a way of doing things, a tradition, and I loved it.

I can't imagine many people saying that make-believe didn't occupy at least some portion of their lives, like it did mine. Put a blanket on your back and you can fly. Sit in a box and race at a hundred miles an hour. Cut out some crudely fashioned piece of construction paper and open up a toy store. It's all there, you just need to make it happen. This was my life for years and years. When Nintendo released the Game Boy, it wasn't exactly something I could just go out and buy at the corner store, so I made my own. All I needed were some paper, a pair of scissors, and a box of colored pencils. With a little cutting work, some expert folding and taping, and some imaginative scenic illustrations, I created my very own portable gaming system, and I didn't even need to change the batteries.

"You gotta believe!"

Now I'm a die-hard Yankees fan, but that catchphrase from the clowns across town really grabbed me. Baseball itself really grabbed me. It had everything I loved all crammed into one sunny summer day.

It had survival! The playoffs. Win or go home. The bottom of the ninth inning. Every single breath counts until it all comes down to a final swing of the bat. It's exhilarating.

It had tradition! This is the sport all Americans were born into. Old-fashioned logos and uniforms have stayed through to modern day, and if anyone even mentioned changing them, a chorus of complaints and empty cans would rain down. Baseball is a game judged by men (in their own traditional uniforms), replete with human error. Not because of a lack of technology, but because of tradition. And the superstitions . . . my god, the superstitions. Don't you dare step on that white chalk line.

It had make-believe! We played baseball, stickball, and Wiffle ball; whatever was manageable with the number of kids around the neighborhood. And we would always skip right to the ninth inning. We would play nine games of all ninth innings, just to feel the excitement of a do-or-die situation. Bottom of the ninth, bases loaded, two outs . . . a last chance at redemption. And the best part was that if you failed, there was another ninth inning coming up right after your three minutes of absolute agony. There was always another chance because make-believe is forever.

Every squad has its own attitude. Its own wrinkled and clumsy face that's seen some shit. A crudely rendered letter or two sewn onto the front of a wool hat and on the chest of a button-down shirt. A nickname hand-carved into the fat side of a splintered club used for bashing and smashing. A wooden bench dug into the ground where you sit, spit, and yell nothing but nonsense, over and over and over again. This is a game where most people don't move for three hours and somehow, thanks to survival, tradition, and make-believe, it's still the most exciting way to spend an afternoon.

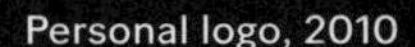
Personal logo, 2010

Branding myself had always been torturous. Hell, branding anything was torturous. But it all clicked when I designed this logo. I realized it's not about designing for what you want something to be, it's about designing for what it is. And it's OK to be metaphorical as long as it communicates a clear message. Did I think anyone was going to confuse me for a baseball team with this logo? No, of course not. What they would assume though is that I probably like baseball, I'm from New York, I'm not afraid to embrace imperfection, and that I enjoy putting a little style into whatever I do, even if it's something as simple as this.

"New York Yankees" doodle, 2010

The original doodle that led to what I consider a major breakthrough in my approach to design and branding. When you draw for a living, sometimes it's easy to forget that you started for fun. This was one of those rare moments I was drawing for fun. It was a single simple thought that opened the door for me. "This was fun to draw . . . it would be cool if I put my name in there instead."

JON CONTINO

Jon Contino

Personal logos, 2010–2013

Various personal brand marks influenced by the style and aesthetic characteristics of baseball

THIS SPREAD & OVERLEAF:
Ebbets Field Flannels, 2013
Clubhouse sweaters

A collection of vintage-inspired baseball designs to mimic clubhouse sweaters and gear from the early days of the sport. Chewing tobacco stains not included.

ND
UB

Giants

LOS ANGELES

LA

BASEBALL CLUB

P.C.L.

NEW YORK

NY

KNIGHTS

BROOKLYN

B.B.C.

New Orleans

29

B. B. CLUB

36

CLUB DE
Royaux
BASEBALL

HOUSE OF DAVID
HD
BASEBALL

SOUTH PHILA
HEBREW ASS'N

OAKLAND

B. B. CLUB

JC
87

Invisible Creature, 2014
Hand-printed bandana and character-progression illustrations for the Seattle-based design studio's baseball-themed product collection

FROM TOP:

Dropbox, 2015, "Dropbox Pro" campaign; Ford, 2013, "And is Better" campaign

Two illustrations inspired by vintage varsity lettering for promotional campaigns

Charlie Hustle

ABOVE:
Charlie Hustle, 2016–2017
Brand icons and logomarks for the Kansas City–based sports-themed clothing brand

OPPOSITE:
FS1, 2017
On-air graphics to kick off the 2017 baseball season on FS1

Boston Red Sox, 2015

"34X34" campaign illustration

An illustration to celebrate the final season of Red Sox slugger David Ortiz—the sort of work a lifelong New Yorker like me could really put his heart and soul into

1234567890

1234567890

ESPN The Magazine, 2014

Sketches and logotypes for the magazine's MLB Preview 2014 issue

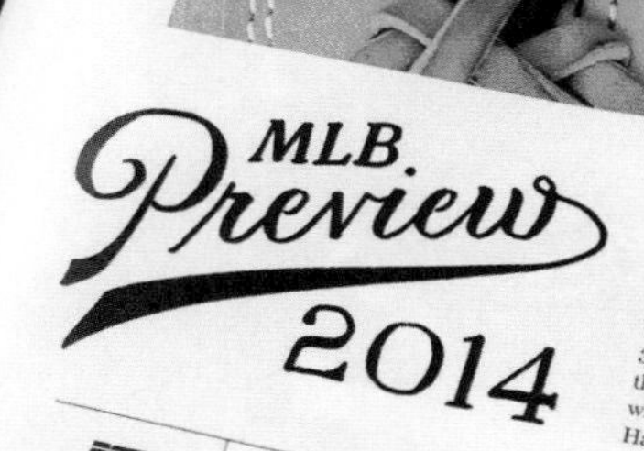

MLB Preview 2014

THIS IS WHAT A GLOVE LOOKS LIKE BEFORE 162 GAMES. T
immaculate yet unweathered. The webbing intricate if
The stitching precise but untested. A fresh glove is at o
a new beginning and a reminder that nothing worth cel
overnight. Not Clayton Kershaw's all-controlling genius
Theo Epstein's latest reclamation project (page 58), or M
37-year journey to the bigs (page 76). As teams chase the
they do so with the knowledge that a lot will change in th
windup to the World Series. Which maybe isn't such a ba
Haven't you heard how long it takes to break one of these

ESPN | 03.31.2014 | COUNTING DOWN TO THE FIRST PITCH? WATCH THE BASEBALL TONIGHT/ESPN THE MLB PREVIEW SHOW ON ESPN ON THURSDAY, MARCH 20, AT 10 P.M. ET

photograph by CHIP LITHERLAND; logos by JON CONTINO

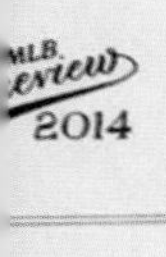

A FAMILIAR ANXIETY *will eat at Clayton Kershaw five hours before his first scheduled start this season. He will pull on a Dodgers cap and the glove he's used for all of his previous outings, grab a baseball and slip outside the door of the unfamiliar clubhouse, alone.*

He will pick out a wall. Any will do. Particulars won't matter as the Dodgers prepare to face the Diamondbacks on March 22 at the retrofitted Sydney Cricket Ground, MLB's first foray into Australia in 100 years. Using a Kershaw-lite version of his mechanics—the mid-delivery pause that deceives hitters, the downward angle, a quick low step toward his target—he will softly short-hop the ball against the base of the wall, catching the ricochet, over and over, the best way he has found to cope with his nervous energy

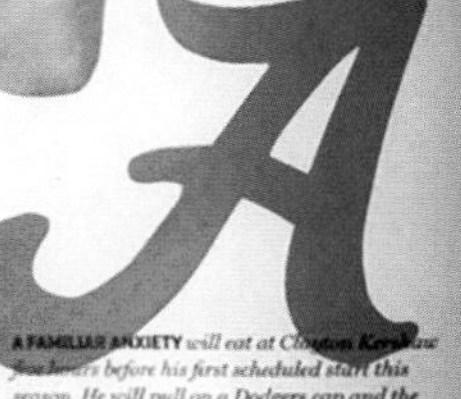

NEW ROYALS COACH MIKE JIRSCHELE SPENT 36 YEARS IN THE BUSHES, MOST OF THEM PREPARING PLAYERS FOR THE JUMP THAT ELUDED HIM. YET HE NEVER BALKED, KNOWING HIS PLIGHT WAS NOTHING COMPARED TO THAT OF HIS THREE BROTHERS.

BY CHRIS JONES | PHOTOGRAPH BY ROB TRINGALI

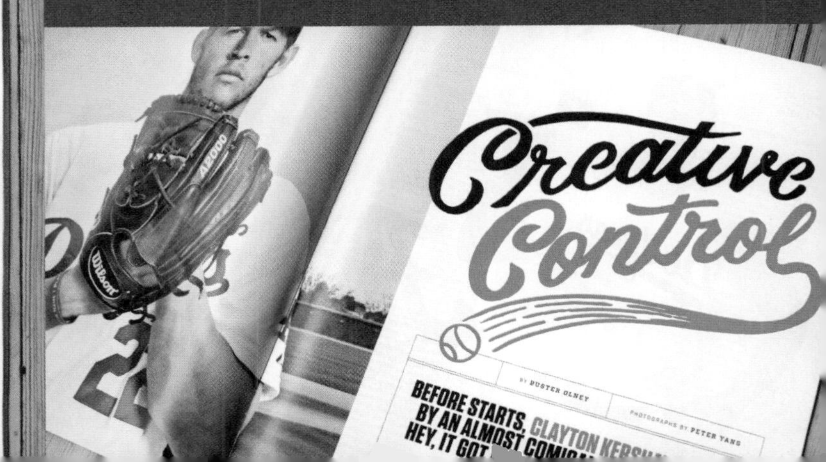

BY BUSTER OLNEY | PHOTOGRAPHS BY PETER YANG

BEFORE STARTS, CLAYTON KERSHAW
BY AN ALMOST COMICAL
HEY, IT GOT

DARING
DF
FIREBALL

DARING
FIREBALL
Est. 2002

DARING
FIREBALL

Daring
FIREBALL

Daring Fireball, 2013–2015

Baseball Collection

Famed tech writer John Gruber commissioned these T-shirt designs for his tech website, Daring Fireball, named in honor of his love for baseball.

MINER
M
LEAGUE

OPPOSITE & FOLLOWING SPREAD:

Miner League, 2016

Logo design for hip-hop-based production company

It's important to remember the journey. Things might appear simple, but the true story is within the process.

MINER
LEAGUE

MINER
LEAGUE

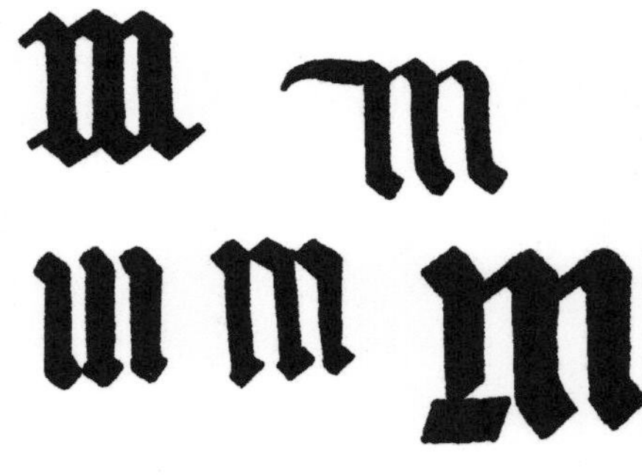

MINER
LEAGUE

MINER
LEAGUE

Miner
LEAGUE
Miner
League
MINER
LEAGUE
MINER
LEAGUE

TOP:
Chicago Wolves, 2016
Commemorative patch

ABOVE & OPPOSITE:
Because Weekend, 2017
Collection illustrations

KING
OF
THE
Diamond

LeatherHead

Leather Head Sports was a company I admired for years, primarily because of the vintage-style leather baseballs they made and the attention to detail that made each ball so special. The only issue I had with the brand was that I felt the logo and packaging were lacking for such a great product.

One day in the spring of 2013, I decided to attempt to make a change for the brand. I called up the founder, Paul Cunningham, and asked him to give me a shot at redesigning the logo. He agreed and let me run with it. When he gave me the green light, I wanted to be sure to put everything I had into creating something memorable for him and his brand. I understood the blood, sweat, and tears that went into making each one of the balls, so I knew it was important to honor that dedication with a meaningful mark.

Flipping through the pages of process sketches, you can actually witness the evolution of the script wordmark—it's pretty wild. But when I look at these pages, I don't think of baseball or lettering. These pages stick in my mind like no other pages in any book. They're a reminder of the hardest week of my life. This particular week I spent driving back and forth to Long Island every day to be with my family and grandmother as she lay in a hospital bed connected to tubes and machines that kept her alive.

After a few days of back and forth, I started sleeping at my parents' house. The long car rides in traffic and long days standing around in hospital rooms began to wear on me. I was also a new dad by just a few weeks, so it was tough leaving my wife and newborn daughter home without me.

My mother set up a temporary bed on the couch in her living room, and I remember sitting there at 2 A.M. with this sketchbook in my lap, slowly drawing script *L*s over and over again until I got just the right one. I don't know how I kept any concentration, but I guess the process kept me preoccupied.

It still kills me to look at these pages, but the memories, good and bad, will forever be sewn into this book. That's something that will never be erased.

LEATHER

- MAIN TYPE
- MONOGRAM
- SCRIPT
- LACE/NEEDL
- "TRADEMARK"

LEA LEATH

LEA

LEATHER HEAD

LEATHER HEAD

Leather Head

Leather Head

Leather Head

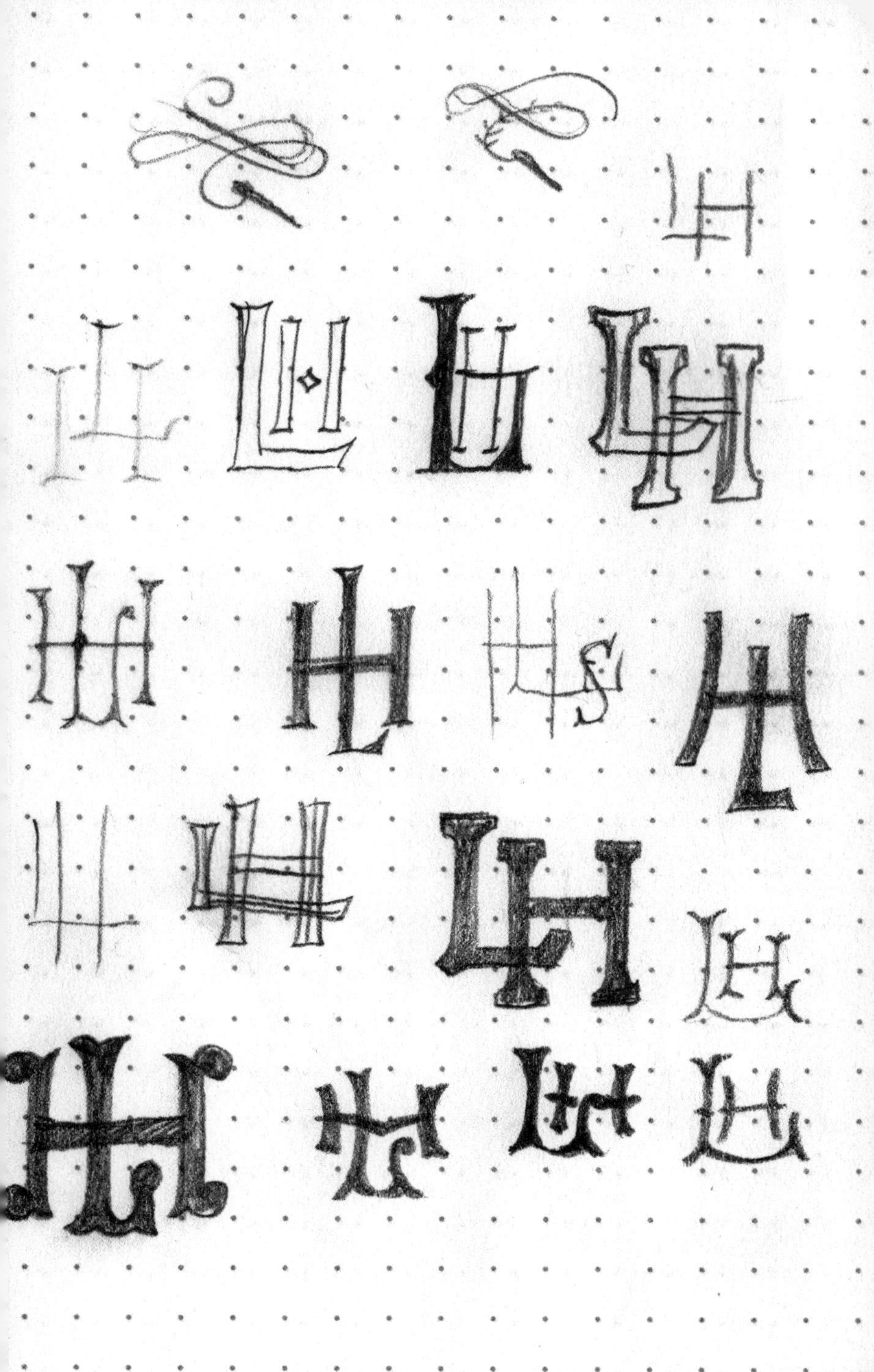

Leather Head
TRADE MARK

LEMON
BASE BALL
PEEL

EXTRAORDINARY
LEMON
BALL
HAND-STITCHED

L H

LH

LEATHER HEAD
SPORTS

LEMON
BASE BALL
PEEL

LEATHER
TRADE MARK
HEAD

Leather Head Sports, 2013–2017
Identity and packaging

MARITIME

The only part of New York City that sits on the mainland of the United States is the Bronx.

And even the Bronx is boxed in by water on three sides, so it's not exactly landlocked. Among Manhattan Island, Staten Island, and Long Island, the majority of the city's inhabitants are all pretty well acquainted with the aquatic life. People here are just as familiar with lighthouses as they are skyscrapers. Boats and ferries are an everyday sight and countless people spend their time on one of the many surrounding bodies of water either for work or pleasure. It's one of those things you don't even think about because it's just a part of the city's DNA. New York is a harbor city, a port city. New York couldn't be New York without the water.

When Matt Gorton and I started CXXVI Clothing Company, we wanted to focus on themes we were most familiar with. We grew up on opposing shores of Long Island, Matt on the north shore and me on the south shore, so there was plenty of local imagery we could pull from as points of reference for the broader narrative. As much as the city was an influence, so was the seafaring life. It seemed like almost everyone owned a boat at some point, even the shittiest little scrap of wood—just as long as it would float, it was good enough. Neighborhood spots were decorated with some kind of anchor or steering wheel hanging on the wall, tangled ropes, a mini lighthouse out front, and paintings of old grimy fishermen. A row of ships always lined the horizon, rickety wooden docks and boardwalks were everywhere, and the personalities that came along with this lifestyle were so intense that they were basically cartoon characters. I mean, New York's being a port city is the whole reason it became the vibrant metropolis it is today—its rich seafaring history is inextricably linked to its modern skyline, and both naturally lent iconography to our work. The visualization of this relationship really is magnetic.

The iconography that comes along with New York's nautical history always appealed to us. Combined, the two settings cover a lot of what I felt drawn to for so many years: visceral music, raw tattoos, hand-scrawled artwork, and a take-no-shit attitude. I can pinpoint each one of those things in various New York "scenes" that I've spent time in, and being able to draw lines from one to the other has allowed for a strong developing narrative in my work. A story told through the rhythms of a sea shanty almost feels like the most memorable way to pass along information. Bone and wood carvings feel like the most permanent documentation of an experience. Self-mutilation and insult-laden brawls as means of passing time seem like no-brainers.

The maritime spirit pulls no punches. The sea is unforgiving—you could easily find yourself lost to the drink for all eternity if you're not careful and quick-witted. "Survival of the fittest" seems like it was coined as a response to this lifestyle, and its inspirational value is as limitless as the sea itself.

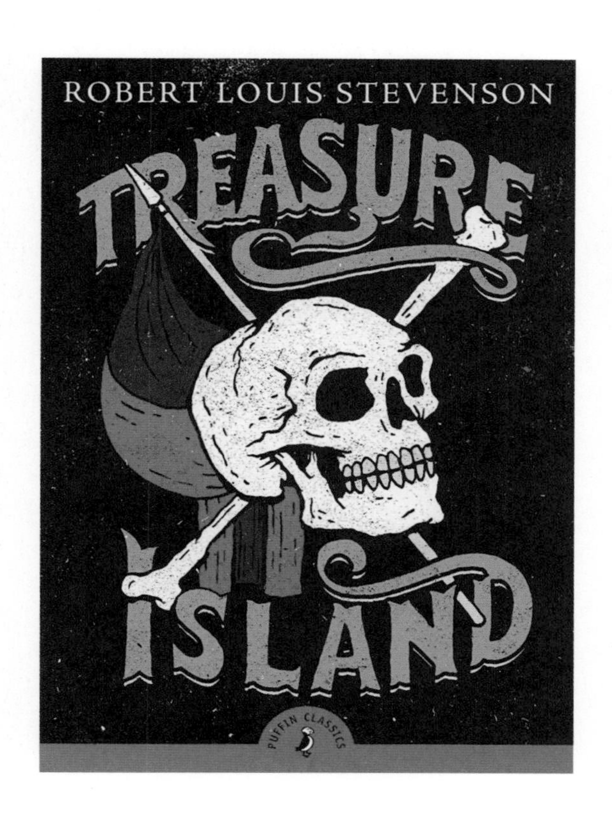

TOP FROM LEFT:

Penguin Classics, 2014, book cover design;

Sarah Lawrence College, 2011, magazine cover design

ABOVE:

Famous Dave's, 2013

Promotional menu design

HURLEY
EST. 1999
BOTTOMS UP

BORN
OF
A
DEEP DARK SEA

LEAVE LUCK ON LAND
RESPECT THE SWELL
GIVE 'EM HELL!
HURLEY

CRUEL SEAS
CAL.
U.S.A.
HURLEY
BURY THE WEAK

RESPECT THE SWELL
HURLEY
GIVE 'EM HELL

Hurley, 2015–2016

"Cruel Seas" apparel series spanning multiple seasons

HERE GOES EVERYTHING
BE THE STORM IN THE CALM
BE THE STORM in THE CALM
BE THE STORM IN THE CALM
HERE GOES EVERYTHING
HERE GOES EVERYTHING
BE THE STORM IN THE CALM
WILD HEARTS TAME SEAS
HERE GOES EVERYTHING
HERE GOES EVERYTHING
BE THE Storm IN THE Calm
WILD HEARTS TAME SEAS
THE SEA'S CALLING ANSWER
HERE GOES EVERYTHING
THE SEA IS CALLING ANSWER

Sperry, 2015
Process sketches

Sperry, 2015

"Seven Seas" branding and campaign illustrations

SEVEN SEAS

HERE
GOES
EVERYTHING

Sperry, 2015

"Seven Seas" concept artwork

SECRET
SOCIETY

"A PICTURE IS WORTH A THOUSAND WORDS."

It may be a cliché, but I think it's pretty much the basis of all branding and logo design. I know it's not really what most mean by the phrase, but it works.

Going back all the way to the cave paintings of Lascaux, images have been one of humankind's best ways of relaying an idea. Who killed the buffalo? Which figure am I supposed to worship? Images become even more powerful when they're reduced to a symbol. Where do I have to stop my car? Where can I go pee? FOR THE LOVE OF GOD WHERE CAN I GO PEE?! The dream of a universal language seems impossible until you remember that symbols exist.

Over the years, the power of symbols has led me to become enamored with logo design. Logos are intentionally designed so that the symbol itself does all the talking, and everyone is supposed to understand what the symbol is saying. As I've studied and learned the history of logos, another type of symbol has crept up and burrowed its way into my brain. Symbols that not everyone knows, symbols you need to have inside knowledge to understand. I'm talking about the symbolism of secret societies.

Who knows how many secret societies are out there, all with their own sets of symbols. Some secret societies are religious, some are antireligious, some may exist for the secret domination of civilization as we know it. Their symbols can be as simple as the letter G (the Freemasons use an uppercase G surrounded by a square and compass) or as ominous as a pyramid with a gigantic eyeball embedded in the middle (known as the "Eye of Providence," found on the back of the dollar bill, and which some claim has a secret meaning). Meeting places for these organizations are extravagantly designed and flooded with symbolism as well. There are beautifully sewn satin banners draped across brass rods hanging behind altars featuring skulls and chain links and various birds, insects, and beasts. Numbers and Latin phrases are chiseled into the sides of massive cement structures. And wherever skulls and Latin are involved, you know cloaks aren't too far behind. Maybe even sacrifices to a lesser-known deity!

But if you break it down to the purest form, a secret society is something we all have had some sort of experience with. Thinking back to the days of playground shenanigans, we had stuff like the "Cool Dudes Club" and the "Totally Awesome Dudes" and the "Radically Cool Awesome Dudes Club for Dudes and Sometimes Girls." Maybe there would be a lightning bolt drawn on a few select notebooks, or a skateboard with a crudely painted skull on the back. Maybe the insignia was just the word "Awesome" surrounded by stars. Whatever it was, you knew what it meant and you were proud to be a part of something, no matter how dumb it actually was.

That grade-school mentality of exclusion, and the love of secret symbols, may explain why secret organizations (that may or may not dominate our world to this day) persist. Some may be evil, or they may not be real at all, but their symbols are something we can all appreciate.

Past Lives, 2016

Chain stitching by Ft. Lonesome, embroidery masters of Austin, Texas

ABOVE FROM LEFT:

B3S, 2014, commemorative flag illustration for the B3S organization; United Pixelworkers, 2012, graphic for the T-shirt brand's "Local" series

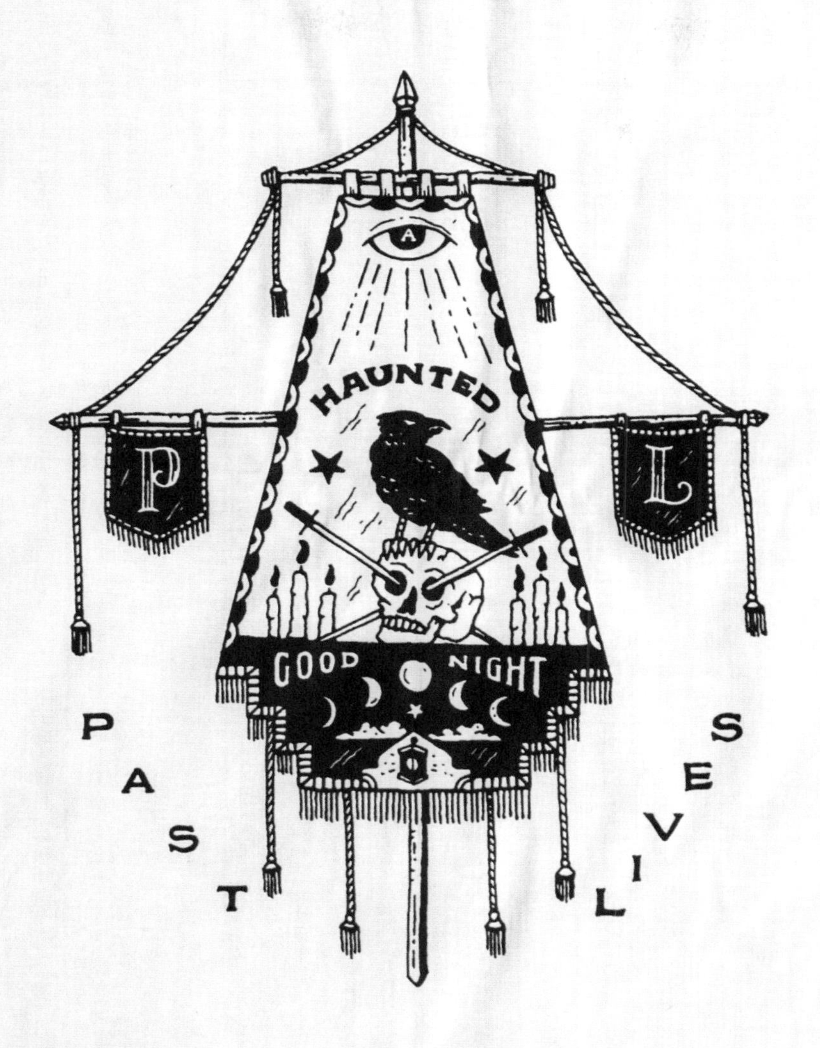

Past Lives, 2015

"A Haunted Good Night" bandana

Forever
RELENTLESS
FOR
TOMORROW
IS
Unknown
GET OVER IT.

THE WHITE COLLECTION
FOREVER RELENTLESS
FOR TOMORROW IS UNKNOWN
GET OVER IT
AETERNE VIVAM

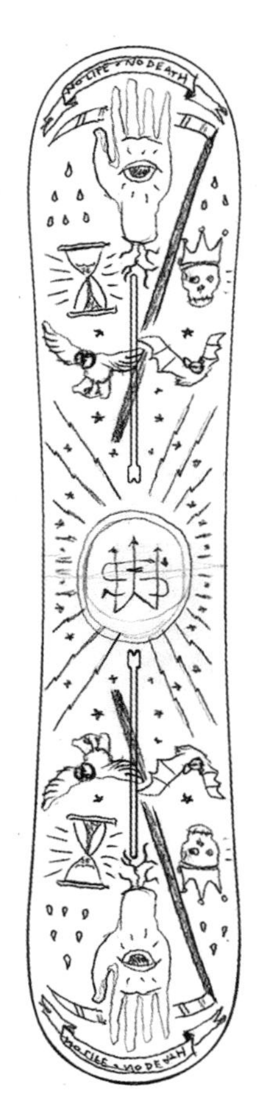
NO LIFE • NO DEATH

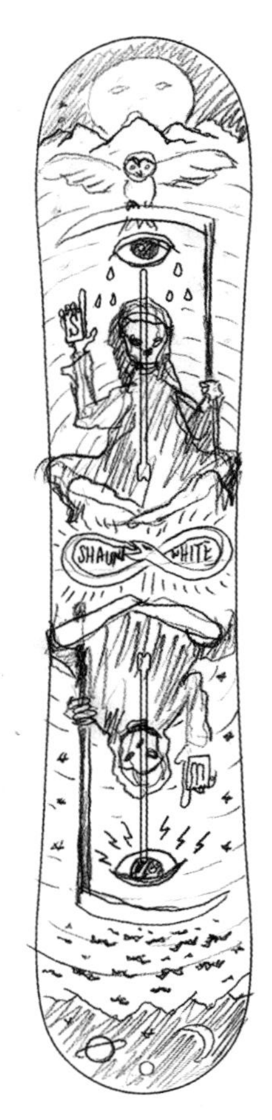
SHAUN WHITE

LIFE IS SHORT · LIVE FAST
LIFE IS SHORT
LIVE FAST

DOOM
FOLLOWS
US
ALL
GET OVER IT.

FEAR NOTHING
FOR FEAR I AM

NO MERCY
NO REGRETS

THE
DEAD
LIGHTS
WATCH

NOTHIN' BUT
BAD LUCK
AND
NO
Regrets
"NAILED IT"

TWC
FEAR NOTHING
FOR FEAR I AM
AETERNE VIVAM
THE WHITE COLL.

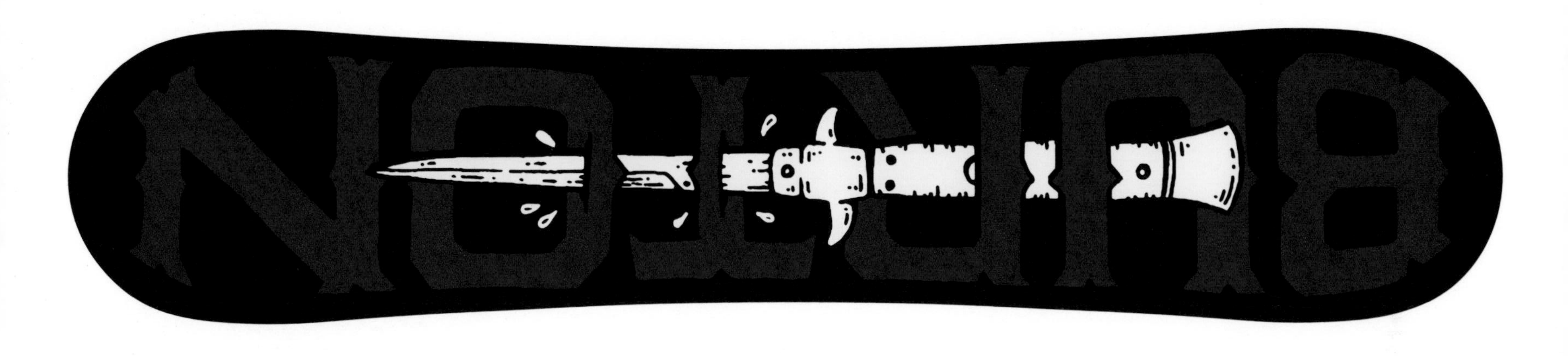

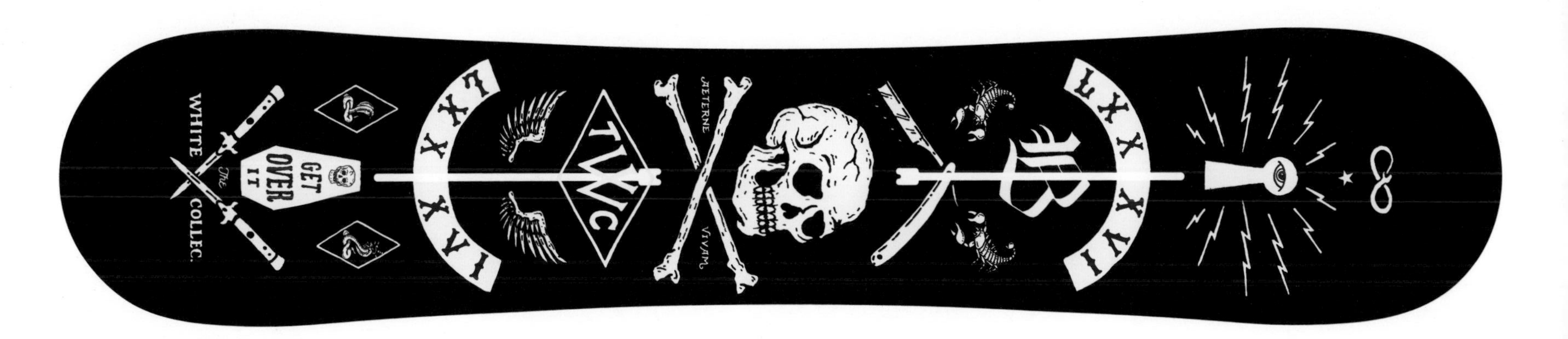

Burton, 2014
"The Shaun White Collection" snowboard design and process illustrations

This single, solitary snowboard design might go down in my personal history as the project with the most revisions. What you see here is merely the tip of the iceberg. This is the kind of job where you start wondering, "Maybe today is the day I finally run out of ideas."

Tattoo

When I was a kid in the 1980s, tattoos were a sign that you were either in jail or going to jail.

There wasn't much of a middle ground. Bikers, tough guys, troublemakers . . . these were the only people who had tattoos. These permanent illustrations were a way to mark yourself so that people knew not to bother you, and if they did, they'd pay for it in one way or another. The older I got, the more fascinated I became by the tattoo culture. I don't think I saw a good tattoo until I was about twenty years old, so I always thought tattoos were just really bad art. Most of what I saw were poorly traced flash, portraits of family members that looked more like dogs, and portraits of dogs that looked like god-knows-what. I never associated any kind of artistic integrity with tattoos, but something still pulled me toward them eventually. That unexplainable pull was one of those primal instincts that makes you hate something on the surface while also being thoroughly intrigued by it deep down.

When a friend of mine from high school mentioned that he liked his tattoos because they told a story of his life, even if they were terrible drawings of bad stories, we laughed about it. But that comment stuck in my head. A few years later, it was still there, and I reexamined what being tattooed meant and what it could look like if I actually put some thought into it.

I agonized over my first tattoo, as most people tend to do. It has to be perfect if this is going on my body forever, I thought. There was a World War II veteran my grandfather was friends with who was covered in tattoos and who was embarrassed by his decision to mark up his skin; he'd always wear as much clothing as possible to make sure not a single line of ink peeked through. But I realized that a lot of choices we make end in permanent—and regrettable—consequences. And that was the exact reason I convinced myself this was something I needed to do. I had it in my head that if da Vinci himself didn't design my first tattoo, it was going to be a complete and utter failure. It's no coincidence that my first tattoo did indeed owe its existence to da Vinci himself: "Art is never finished, only abandoned." I figured that was a safe bet. A quote I lived my life by, said by an artist I worshipped, in a spot that was easy to hide, even by a T-shirt. But then came the itch, and one became two, and two became four, until I became a dedicated tattoo collector. I have plenty of friends who still mock me every time I get a new tattoo: "I thought you hated tattoos." Whatever. Leave me alone. I changed my mind, OK?!

I have friends who have gone through a similar process and it has been great fun to swap stories of how and why we got our tattoos, share ideas for cool ink, and talk about what we have planned for the future. Oh, and to laugh at one another when one of us makes a really bad choice that we know we'll regret at some point. But that is the gamble that makes a bad tattoo good and a great tattoo even better. Through all of this, I learned how the power of art and illustration is one of the strongest possible ways to tell a story.

Tattoos are the most elemental story art, inscribing ideas onto our bodies. And not just the tattoos we know today, but also those of native cultures going back thousands of years. Marking and scarring one's body figuratively and literally symbolizes a change in that person. I realized that all those bad tattoos I hated so much still give great value to a person's life story. In fact, they seem kind of amazing now. To be tattooed on a ship somewhere in the Pacific Ocean, thousands of miles away from home, by a guy who smuggled some ink on board to draw a weird-looking hula girl. To be tattooed in a jail cell by someone who could just as well break you into pieces. To be tattooed by a friend experimenting with body modification for no other reason than "My mom is working late." These are pretty general tattoo clichés that most people seem to attribute to a throwaway culture, but there's so much more to it than that. The psychology behind these clichés casts a rich and vibrant story, one that gives us a deeper look into who we are as people and how we feel about the choices we make. Tattoos document the human experience.

I realize now after years of collecting tattoos that hating on tattoo culture is like calling the cave paintings of Lascaux "shitty doodles." Tattoos aren't about the quality of the illustrations, but what they represent—the stories they tell and how the artist was able to tell them. Like modern art, which is often viewed with an "I could do that!" mentality, tattoos are a study in process and frustration and composition, and not necessarily beauty and perfection. It's struggle and emotion and free will, and it's amazing.

Many artists will talk about loosening up with sketches or doodles to start the day, but that's never worked for me. My relentless determination to complete tasks and move on to the next thing keeps me from having anything to do with the word "loose."

However, every now and then the mood will strike me to "get loose" and do something weird. Having little to no restrictions is nice for this kind of thing.

For the above illustrations, I collected a bunch of

paper for customers to choose from) and attempted to recreate each one without lifting the brush pen off the page. I kept my eyes up and pen down, only stopping when I felt an illustration was complete.

A lot of these aren't pretty, or legible for that matter, but you'll always learn something new about yourself when you get completely uncomfortable. I can say that exercises like this one always help me to remember that keeping things loose also helps to keep them fun and interesting.

"FLASH" LIGHTS

FIRST EDITION

DOOMED

1. "DOOMED"

2. "CROW SKULL"

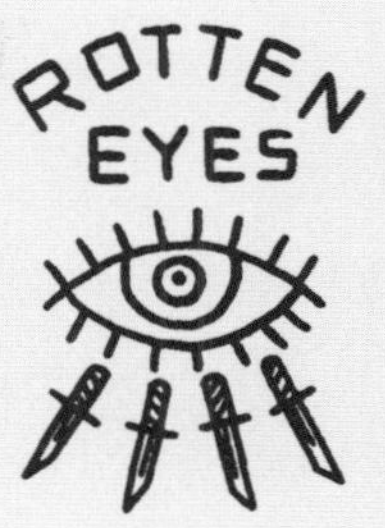

3. "ROTTEN EYES"

4. "ROSE"

5. "RATTLESNAKE"

6. "RABBIT"

DEAD END
RELENTLESS
DEATH

DO OR DIE
Lucky No 13
WATCH YOUR BACK!
Bad Luck...
I'd have
None.!
DISHONOR !

ABOVE & PREVIOUS SPREAD:
Journal Standard, 2016
Furniture design

DEAD END
RELENTLESS
U CAN'T FIGHT FATE
ENDLESSLY DOOMED
if it wasnt fo
Bad Luck...
I'd have None!
DO OR DIE
Lucky No. 13
WATCH YOUR BACK!

ABOVE FROM LEFT: Lucky Brand, 2013; personal illustration, "Born Free," 2010

Initially drawn as a tongue-in-cheek, patriotic knockoff of Blake Hampton's incredible "Joe Levine Unchained" illustration, which was featured in *Esquire* magazine in 1961, the "Born Free" Uncle Sam led to a personal series of tattooed-strongman illustrations that became the perfect canvas to showcase tattoo-style illustration in the context of the human body.

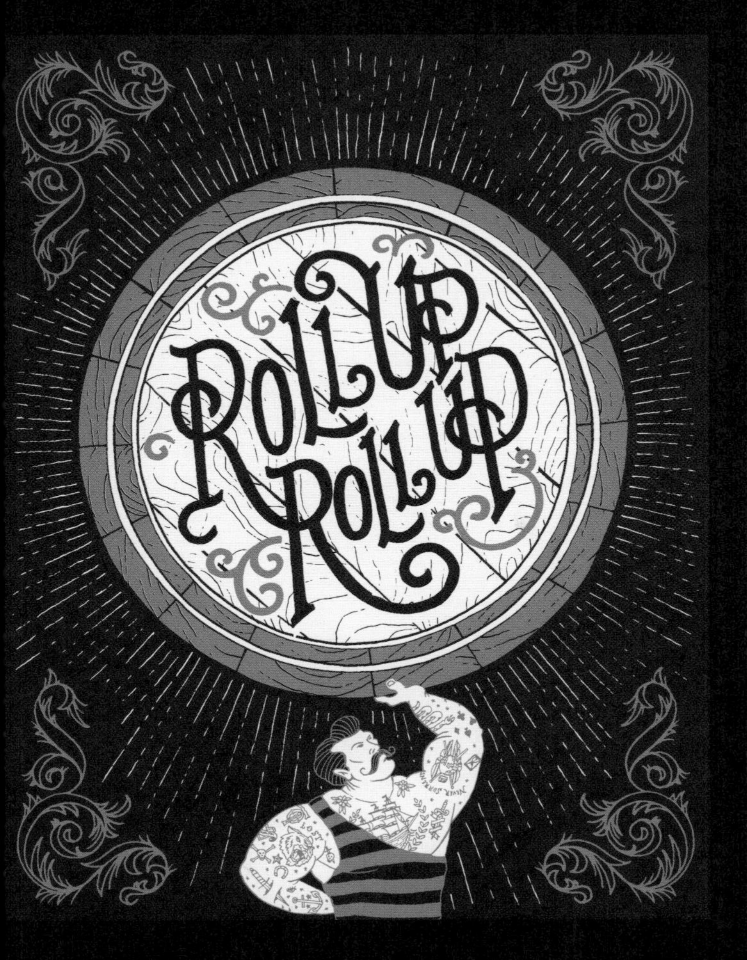

TOP FROM LEFT:
One Tun, 2015, pub signage; Whole Foods, 2012, cover illustration for holiday mailer

ABOVE:
20th Century Fox, 2017
Deadpool 2 promotional illustrations for Brazil Comic Con

OCTOBER 2014

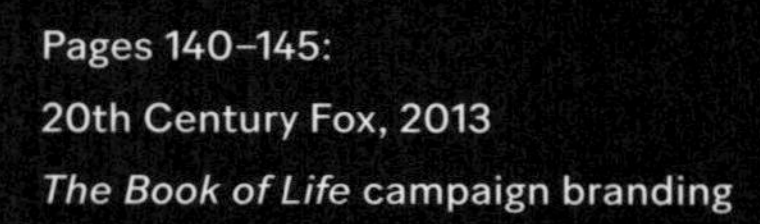

Pages 140–145:
20th Century Fox, 2013
The Book of Life campaign branding

A vast collection of posters, logos, and icons, including a custom font, to promote the release of Jorge Gutierrez's animated film *The Book of Life*. It was vital for me to produce each item with the most authentic Mexican aesthetic possible. I may have spent more time researching and learning about Mexican culture than actually drawing for this project. When all was said and done, I received a message from Jorge that read, "I can't believe you're not Mexican!"

The
BOOK of LIFE
2014
XXX

The
Book
of
Life

The
"Book of Life"

THE
BOOK
of
LIFE

THE BOOK OF LIFE

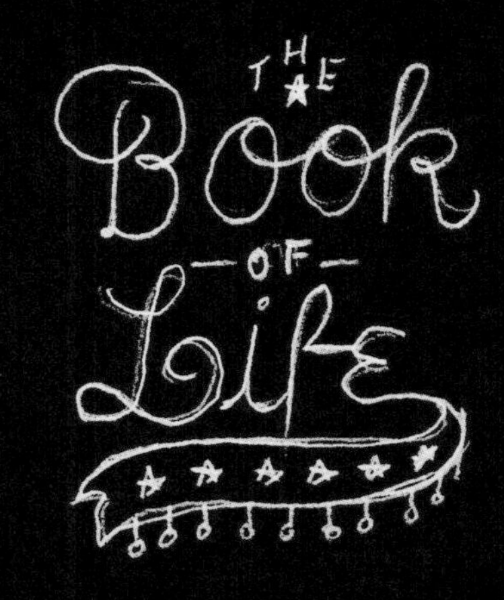

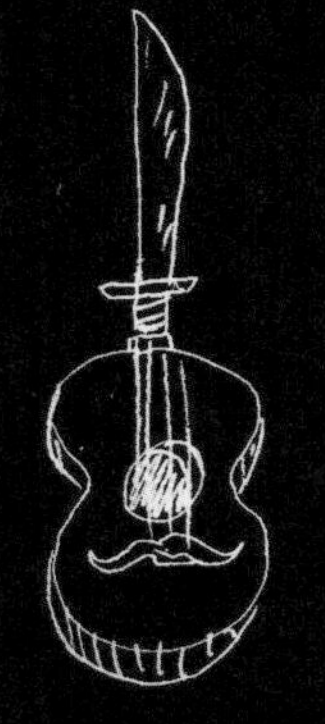

ABCDE

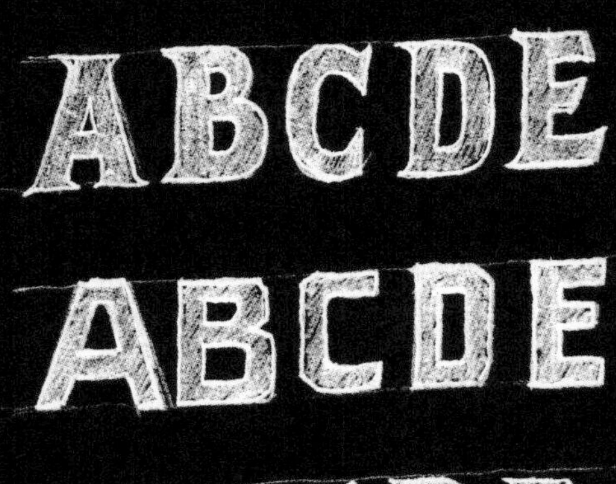

ABCDE

ABCDE ABC

ABCDE

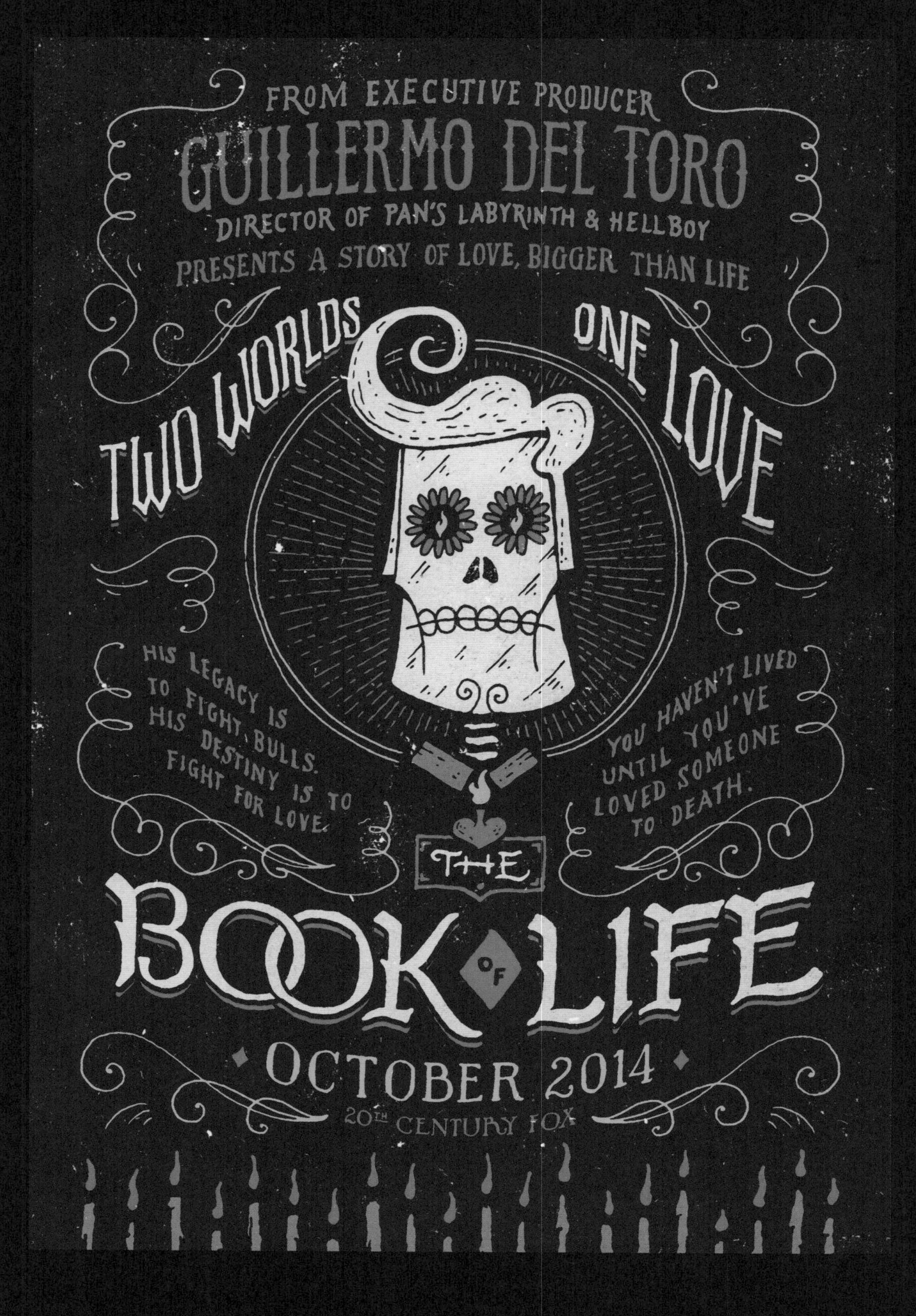
FROM EXECUTIVE PRODUCER
GUILLERMO DEL TORO
DIRECTOR OF PAN'S LABYRINTH & HELLBOY
PRESENTS A STORY OF LOVE, BIGGER THAN LIFE
TWO WORLDS
ONE LOVE
HIS LEGACY IS TO FIGHT BULLS. HIS DESTINY IS TO FIGHT FOR LOVE.
YOU HAVEN'T LIVED UNTIL YOU'VE LOVED SOMEONE TO DEATH.
THE
BOOK OF LIFE
OCTOBER 2014
20TH CENTURY FOX

the
BOOK of LIFE

ABCDEFGHIJKLMN
OPQRRSTUVWXYZ
0123456789 ? ! ¿¡
ËĒÍÑ

AFTER DARK

I'm going to let you in on a little secret:

As I write these very words, it's currently 3:24 A.M. and I am engulfed in pitch-black darkness.

Since I was a young boy, maybe nine or ten years old, I have often found myself awake and ambitious in the middle of the night. From watching MTV's *Headbangers Ball* and terrible infomercials, to the early days of the internet and chat rooms, I've always flourished in the witching hour. The synapses in my brain almost feel like they're firing faster and more accurately. Everything just clicks.

Throughout the day, there are too many distractions. The demands of relationships, the pull of technology, the latest news, the hot gossip, whatever. We're all being pulled in a million different directions. But once the sun goes down and everyone is in bed, a calm comes over the world that could never exist in our sunlit lives. In the middle of the night . . . oh, that's when the magic happens.

That's when the brain kicks into overdrive. The analytical part goes to bed, and the creative side can take over.

The "Witching Hour Vacuum," as I like to call it, creates a very interesting person. When a normal human wakes up at 3:30 A.M., it's usually not a good thing—the culprit is either sickness, panic, or something in between. The person who falls outside of these boundaries is something I like to call the "All-Nighter." This is another creature entirely. While everyone sleeps, the All-Nighter creeps around the hallways. The All-Nighter flourishes in a dead world. The All-Nighter maneuvers through space while everything remains silent and steady—free to roam without interference.

Some of my best and most interesting work has been produced in the middle of the night. It allows me to be inside my head and poke around at what my brain can do instead of having to worry about getting things done in between phone calls, meetings, and family life.

For me, the midnight shift is a path back to a child's limitless wonderment and ability to problem-solve, without prejudice or fear of judgment. The dark, quiet freedom of night eliminates all senses of embarrassment. It's the perfect incubator for my strangest observations and most outrageous concepts—the ideal place to finally cultivate something unique outside of a bloated and frustrating daytime schedule.

ALL NIGHTER

MOON TOOTH CHROMAPARAGON
QUEEN WOLF / OFFERED BLOOD / IGNEOUS / LITTLE WITCH / BATS IN THE ATTIC / FORGIVE ME SNAKE RYDER / CHROMA
VESUVIUS I / VESUVIUS II / BELT SQUEEZER / DEATH AND THE VIBRANT ARCHITECTURE OF REBIRTH / WHITE STAG

CHROMA PARAGON
MOON TOOTH

OPPOSITE:
Moon Tooth, 2015
Chromoparagon album artwork, logo design, and concept sketches

TOP LEFT:
Beams, 2015
Collaborative collection tagline graphic for the Japanese clothing brand

TOP RIGHT, ABOVE:
Lucky Brand, 2015
Collaborative collection illustrations

ENSAMBLE

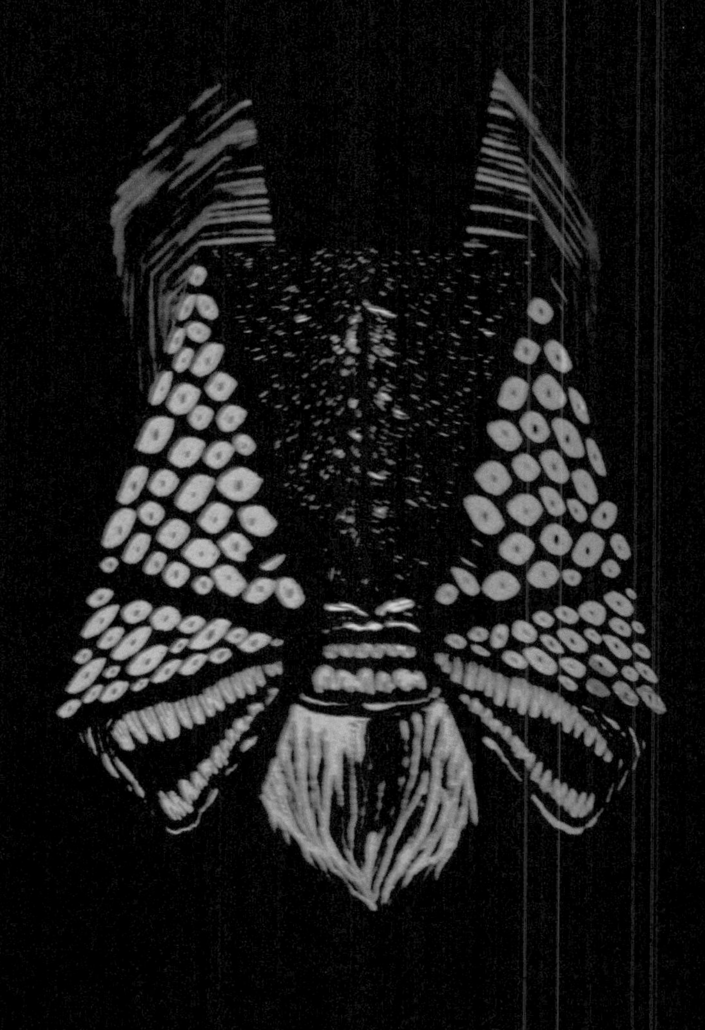

"Night Terror," 2016

3-D glow-in-the-dark paper mask

This mask was exhibited in *Mr. Rabbit Collection*, a group art show curated by Proyecto Ensamble of Santiago, Chile. The design was printed on cardboard with a few die-cuts and folding lines so that it could be transformed into a three-dimensional, wearable mask. I wanted this thing to be creepy. Like, really creepy. So, I added a hundred eyes and some weird old-man teeth, made the fur on the snout part in an upside-down cross, and wrote "Night Terror" on the back. The fact that the mask glows in the dark brought all of that to life in a fun and unsettling way.

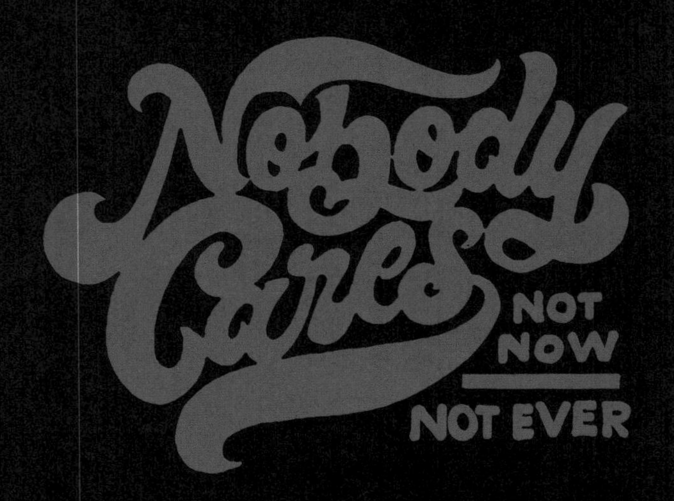

NO WINNERS

KILL

ONLY

SURVIVORS

NORTH AMERICAN

SILK

SCREENERS

+ SOCIETY +

EST. 1981

"BORN WITH BLISTERS"

OPPOSITE:
JCNYC, 2016

ABOVE LEFT:
PinZilla, 2016
Enamel pin and backing card design
for a traveling lapel-pin exhibition

ABOVE RIGHT:
JCNYC, 2017

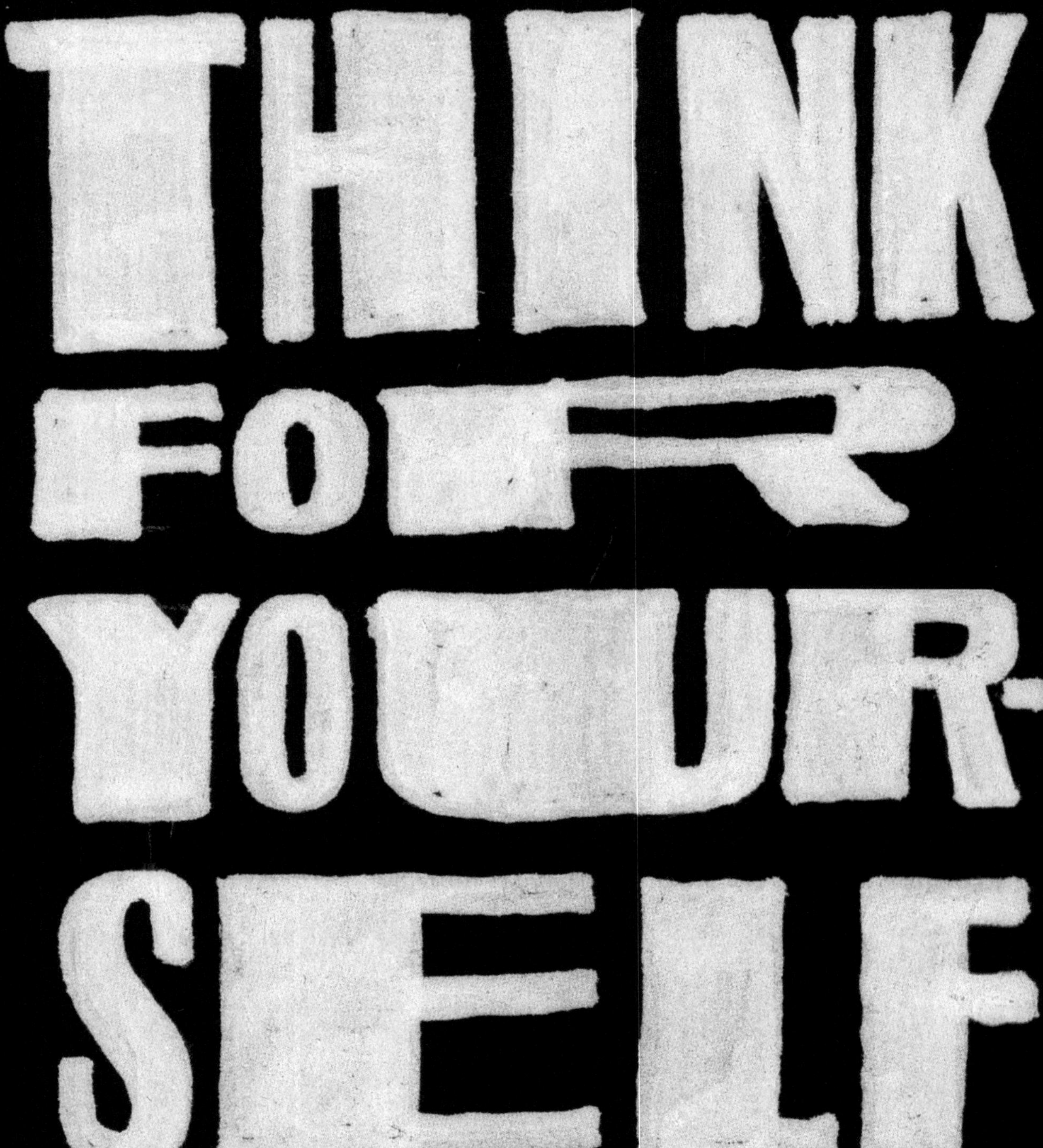

THINK
FOR
YOUR-
SELF

Personal illustration, 2016

BORN 2
FRY

WHEN IN
ROME
...GET NASTY

N.Y.C. FOREVER
J. Contino

J. Contino

J. Contino
Lazy
Day

POSSESSIONS
Free!
For
All
Eternity
WHILE-U-WAIT
J. Contino

FIRST AMENDMENT
DEATH TRAP
J. Contino

SATANS
SINNER
SEWING
CLUB

TELL THIS
FORTUNE!
J. Contino

MAGIC
O
K
J. Contino

J. Contino
Norman Rockwell
American Her

IF I DIE BEFORE
I WAKE,
I HOPE YOU
GET BITTEN
BY A SNAKE.
J. Contino

GO
HOME
J. Contino

Skull-caP
J. Contino

YES!

Yo!

No!

BORING

NOPE

HEY

GET LOST

SERIOUSLY?!

EHHHH...

UGHHH

YEAH RIGHT

SooYa!

Amazing

No Regrets

THIS IS GARBAGE

H MY
GOD

Thank You

NO
THANKS

O.K.

NOBODY
CARES

BIG
DEAL

AWESOME

GOOD
NIGHT

BITE ME

THIS
RULES

IT'S
TIME

R.I.P.

#1

NEWS
THIS
JUST IN

ALL SIGNS POINT TO
8
WHATEVER

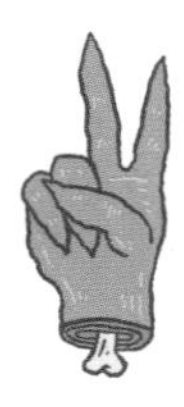

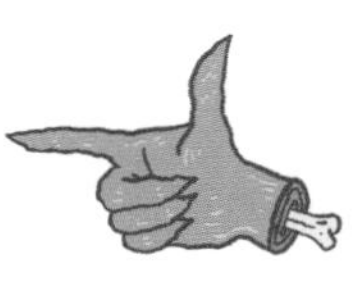

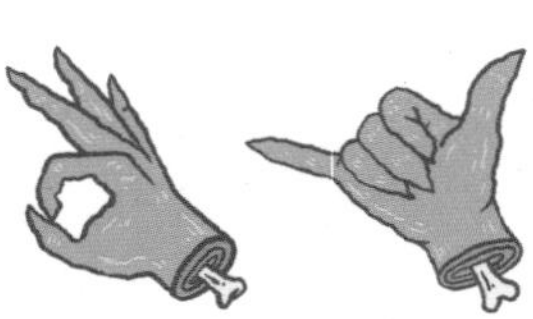

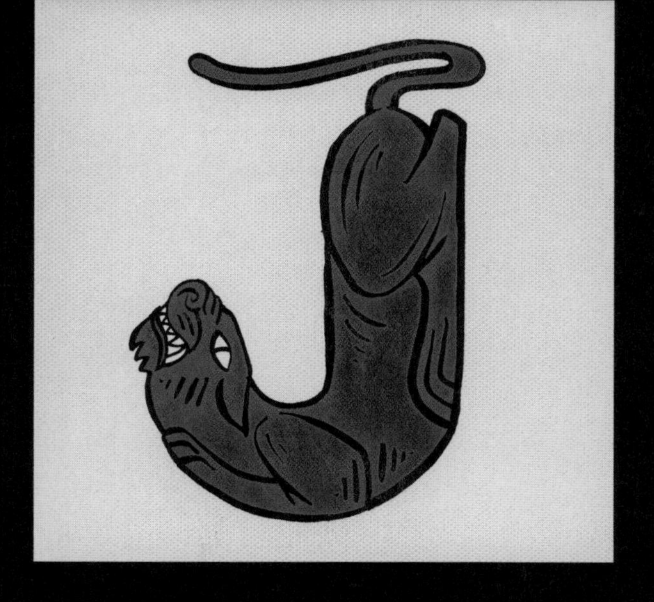

OPPOSITE:
"The Nose Knows," 2016
Basically a replacement for emoji, these illustrated messages and icons were part of a custom Apple Messages sticker collection. Fun fact: The "nose" in question is an inside joke within my family. A good portion of us have big Italian noses, and we enjoy pointing this out any chance we get. If you notice references to noses in any of my other work, now you know why.

ABOVE:
Various personal illustrations, 2015–2016

BORN
FREE

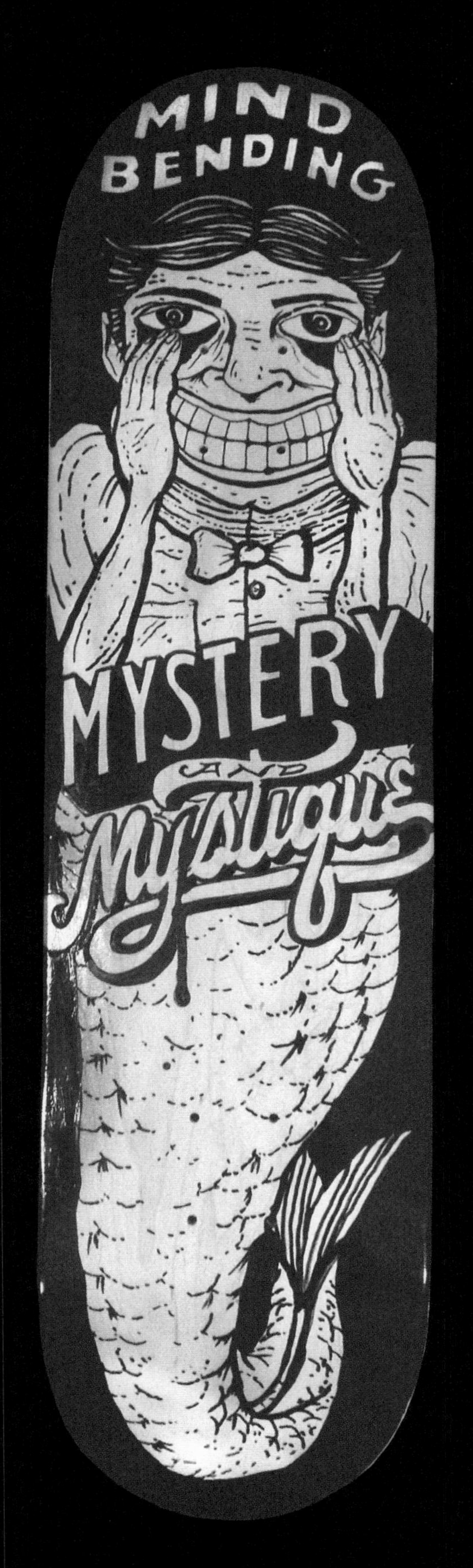

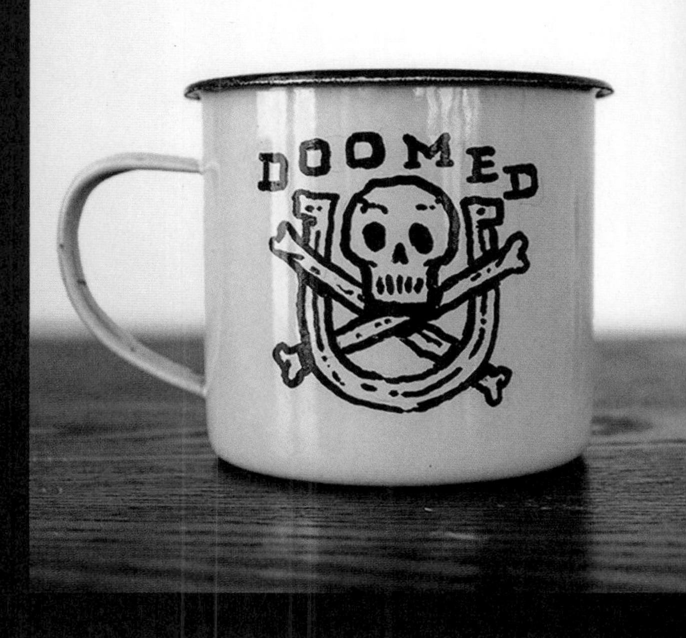

OPPOSITE, CLOCKWISE FROM TOP LEFT:

Past Lives, 2015

Ride On PDX, 2013
Hand-painted skateboard deck

Personal illustration, 2013

ABOVE:

Past Lives, 2015
Hand-painted enamel mugs

At the most you'll feel my ghost
on some quiet mild evening.

Don't be afraid
she's almost saved
from all the earthly grieving.

Quietly don't make a sound
on those old creaky floor boards.

Up the stairs
she's almost there.
no need to turn the light on.

Louie boy, oh Louie baby
so sweet, so sweet my darling

Your blue eyed stare
the clothes you wear
can be so very charming.

Then that one night, the moon light bright
you brought me to the river.
The ropes so tight without a fight,
your strenghth it over-took me.

Down I fell, into a hell
so deep, so dark, so empty.
I couldn't win
the water sucked me in
and here I'll stay forever.

But you my dear stood laughing there
upon the rocks just watching.

What did I do
What did I say
to make you end our date this way?

ABOVE:

"Haunts: A Collection of Gothic Yarns," 2015

Illustrated short stories about ghostly encounters, written by Erin Contino

OPPOSITE:

Past Lives, 2016

PAST
LIVES
A
DARKENED
MID-NIGHT
BREEDS
MIS-
FORTUNE

HARD X CORE

When I heard the first scream over a distorted guitar,

I knew I had found something I could identify with—or, at the very least, use for a quick minute to vent whatever frustrations I had.

It all began around 1996 when I was in the seventh grade. I remember a good friend of mine let me borrow his brother's band's demo. The band was called Overthrow, and they were a local hardcore act that had a pretty significant presence in Long Island. At this point in my life, the bands that played in front of thirty people had the same star power as those selling out a stadium for a week. That was my perception at least; I had no idea what I was getting into. Within a year or two I was spending every weekend (and a lot of weeknights) at clubs in Long Island, Queens, and Manhattan following all my favorite bands from night to night. The internet was just a baby at the time, so the only way I could ever find out about a show was by getting a flyer at another show, and I'd leave it next to my bed at home to make sure I didn't miss anything. This is where the whole can of worms opens up.

I need to break this down, because there's so much about the world of hardcore that had a significant impact on me.

We have the music, that's number one. Raw, aggressive, emotional, and sloppy as hell. There were no rules to play by, no one judging you, and no promoters to make you feel worthless. If you had something to say and somewhere between two and four people to back you up with sounds of any kind, you had a place to play. In order to be successful, you had to actually give a shit about what you were doing. You couldn't coast through the hardcore scene and just expect anything in return. In order to receive, you had to give. Stepping outside of normal society and into this world was like being dropped on another planet. It was OK to scream and even more OK to beat the shit out of your instruments and your friends; in fact, it was encouraged. Just about the last thing you'd want to do is hold back at a hardcore show. That would be like going to a five-star restaurant and just having a glass of water.

Then there was the community: a collection of aimless kids from different backgrounds, ethnicities, family lives, and belief systems. The hardcore scene was the first place I ever really felt normal for once. To be clear, I never really had much trouble in school. I was generally a pretty smart kid, with no behavioral issues, who was pretty decent in sports and art, and always got along well with everyone. And yet, I still felt like I didn't belong. At hardcore shows, I was surrounded by people I never expected to connect with, but the scene became my home away from home almost instantly. It was a self-governing community that took care of itself. When there was a fight, it was settled. When someone was in trouble, they were helped. A series of unspoken ethical guidelines allowed all of these weird people to coexist and even flourish. This was a place where you could fall down while breaking someone's nose, and the person whose nose you broke would help you back to your feet. It was a place that held benefit shows to pay for someone's medical or legal bills. It was a place where hopeless drug addicts and vegan health fanatics saw eye to eye and no one was judged for their life choices. We all knew that what we were there for was bigger than each one of us, and we cherished it. That's not something you get in a "normal" day, and you'd better believe we clung to it for dear life.

Then, of course, there was the art. A community of untethered youth playing loud, abrasive music while beating the shit out of each other spawned an incredible aesthetic. With no money and no formal training, an entire art form basically sprung up on its own. Demos, T-shirts, flyers, posters, stickers, patches, all of it needed to be designed. Some kids figured out how to screen print, others were graffiti masters and offered up their services to design logos, and others knew how to manipulate pictures with a ten-cent photocopy. An entire ecosystem of graphic design developed without anyone even knowing what the hell graphic design was. The hardcore scene even followed the same trend cycles as mainstream design. For example, around 1999 or so, everyone wanted a demo cover with their band's name set in a script typeface with ellipsis dots following the name. I guess this represented thought? I don't know. I don't know if anyone ever knew why they wanted it; they just thought it was cool. Then came the graffiti days, the varsity days, the metal days. Music and art trends went hand in hand, and the hardcore scene and design community influenced each other and built upon whatever style was currently booming until it got played out and someone broke the mold again.

That brings me to the entrepreneurial aspect of the hardcore scene. Bands needed to sell stuff in order to make more stuff, so without realizing it, each band became a small business, and at every show there were at least one or two "distros" (distributors). These were people who brought milk crates full of records, tapes, and CDs for sale. They had stuff from bands you'd never heard of from places you didn't know existed. It was a time before instant information, so you had to rely on what a record cover looked like and what the distro seller had to say about it. I remember picking up a tape from a band in Virginia called Destined to Fail solely on the recommendation of the guy behind the table. I don't know if anyone had ever heard of this band before (or after) that moment, but that tape had some of my favorite songs. Oh, and I can't forget the hardcore record shops either. These places usually existed only because their primary source of revenue was selling piercings or adult entertainment. I knew no other media outlets would ever bother to carry this stuff, and I always wondered if the maniac behind the counter even knew what records he was buying for the back of the store. A lot of these places didn't last too long either, probably because they were catering to a demographic with almost no money, but we still went anyway and made wish lists based on word of mouth and cover design, and then migrated to the next shop once the last one closed.

The world of the underground hardcore scene in New York still affects me to this day. I remember feeling like I had found the fountain of youth when I discovered the hardcore community, and I wasn't even sixteen yet. I always thought it was a great representation of what the city stood for: a bunch of misfits finding common ground and setting up shop wherever it was possible. It really made you feel like you'd be invincible forever. Even now I can pop on an old Indecision or VOD record and feel like I could knock down an entire building by myself. As I age, it becomes clear that my days of discovering something this raw and powerful become less and less likely. There's a big part of me that feels deeply scarred and saddened that I'll never have that moment of discovery again, but goddamn if that wasn't one of the single greatest moments in my life.

Indecision, 2012
Shirt design for the legendary Brooklyn hardcore band

Exfm, 2011

Spot illustration for the now-defunct music service

Incendiary, 2012

Shirt design for one of the most popular current hardcore bands

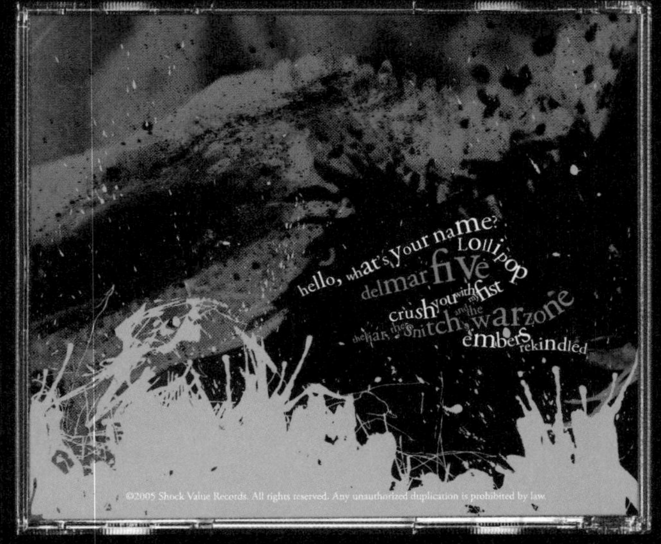

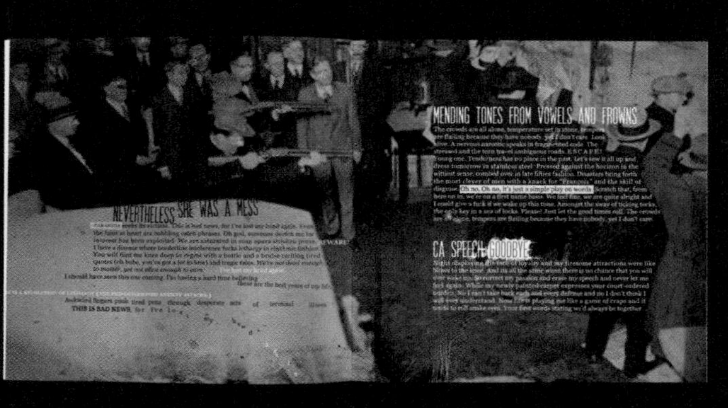

TOP:
The Ambition, 2005
A Legacy of Ruin EP

ABOVE:
Anterrabae, 2003
Shakedown Tonight LP

For most of the late 1990s and early 2000s, I spent my time designing music packaging for hardcore bands and indie record labels. I thought designing for the music industry was going to be my ticket to easy street . . . until the iPod came out. Thanks, Apple.

AT HISTORY'S END

AT HISTORY'S END

LAST PERFECTION DRAWING CONCLUSIONS

8 80270 02342 4
1 THE INCEPTION
2 EVERYONE IS A POET
3 IRONY IS NOT THE WORD
4 GOOD NIGHTS, BAD MORNINGS
5 WALKING A MILE IN CEMENT SHOES
6 OBTUSE AND OBSCURE
7 1128
8 WHAT A PITY
9 THE NUMBER 5 LOOKS LIKE 2
UNITED EDGE RECORDS
© & ℗ 2004 UNITED EDGE RECORDS
WWW.UNITEDEDGE.COM

TOP: ABOVE:

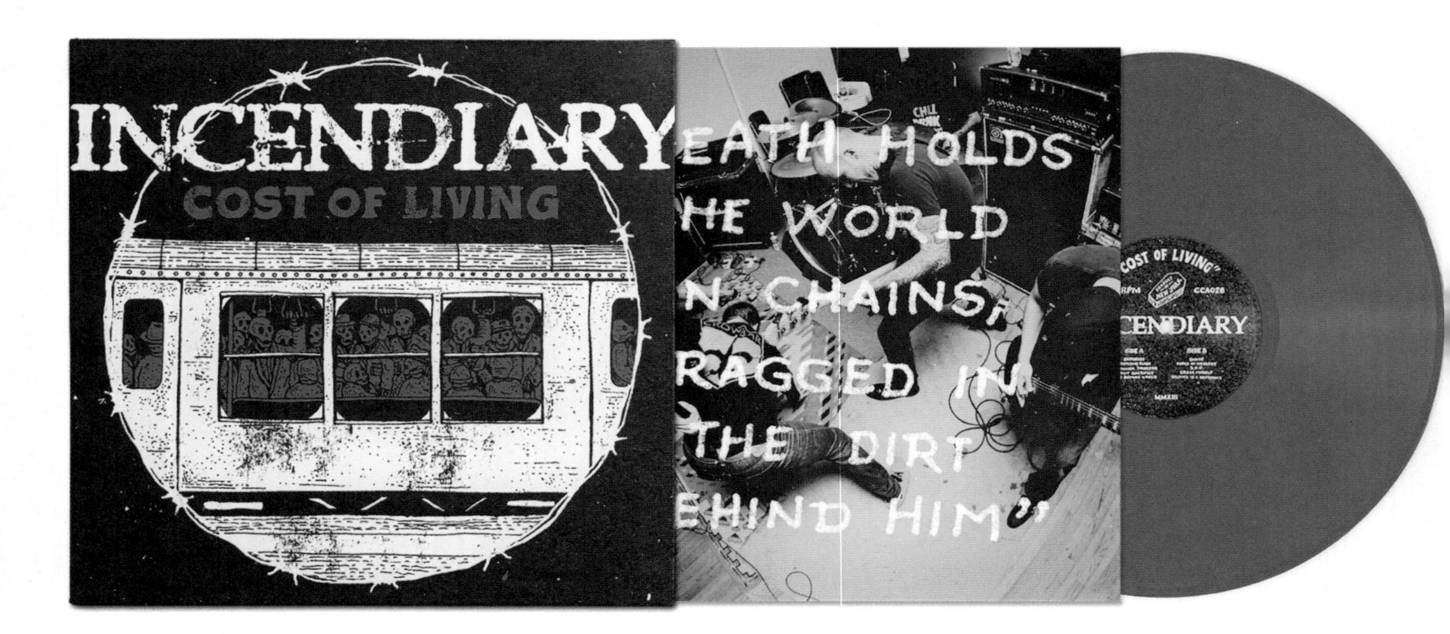

Incendiary, 2012
Cost of Living LP

These days, designing albums for hardcore bands is strictly about having fun and keeping in touch with my roots. Plus, everyone went back to vinyl, which is awesome. CD jewel cases were the worst.

Side A
Victory in Defeat / God's Country
Side B
Drifter / Land of the Lost
Closed Casket
Activities

Incendiary/Suburban Scum, 2013
Split 7" reissue

Fireburn, 2017
Don't Stop the Youth EP

Layout, type, and logo design for a band that features some past and present hardcore legends

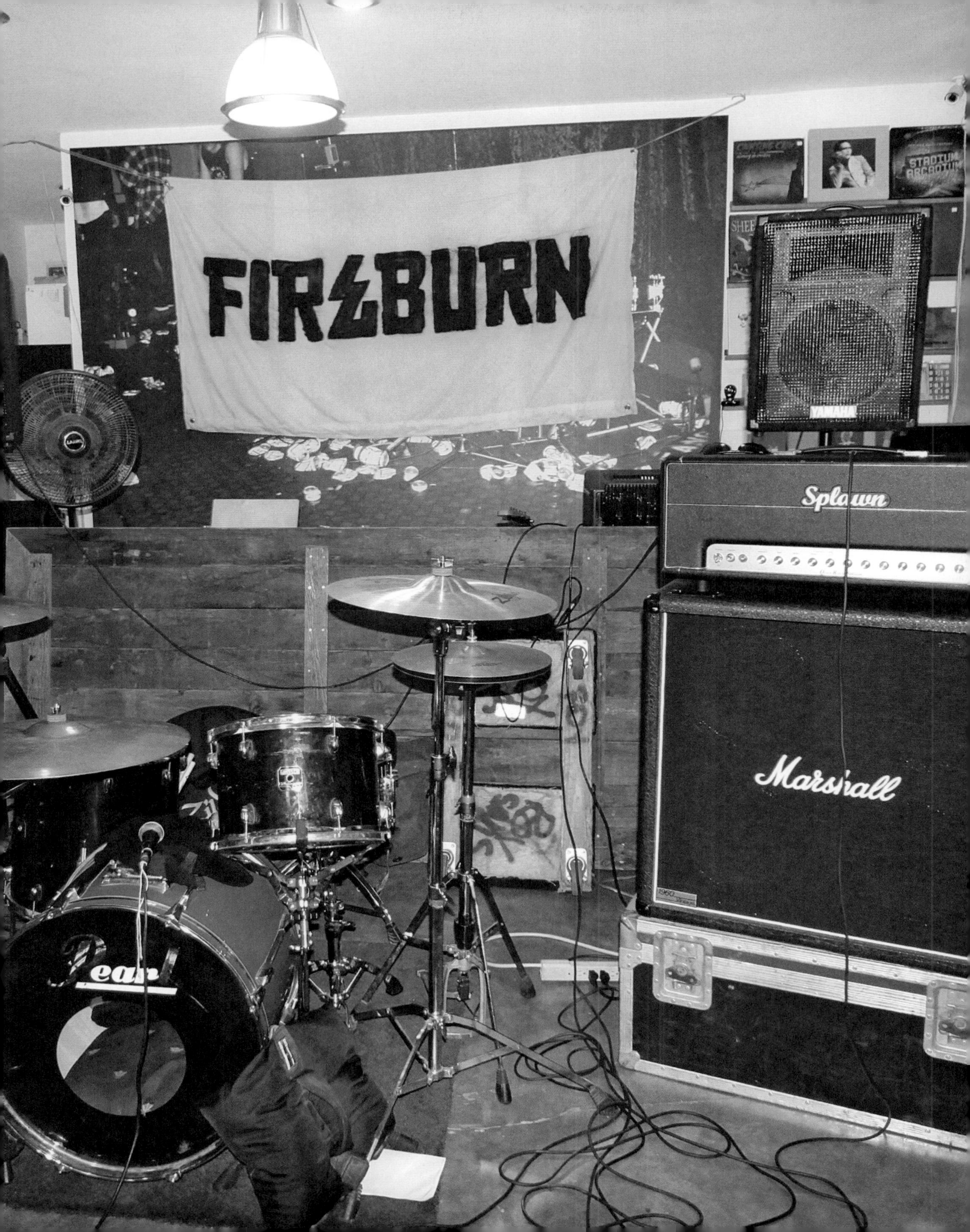
YAMAHA
Splawn
Marshall

HORROR

I SPENT THE MAJORITY OF MY CHILDHOOD BEING TERRIFIED OF WEREWOLF ATTACKS.

Seriously. Not home invasion or mugging, not being kidnapped by a creep in a van with a bunch of great candy, not even having my parents die and then being sent to a nineteenth century–style orphanage. Just werewolf attacks. It took me almost two decades to finally sit down and watch the werewolf transformation scene in *An American Werewolf in London*. Hell, even the scene in *The Sandlot* where "The Beast" jumps through the movie screen that's showing an actor in a cheesy werewolf costume prompted immediate fast-forwarding on the VCR. I can't really pinpoint when that fear actually started and where it came from, but it had some serious staying power. I remember looking at wedding venues with my fiancée-now-wife, Erin, and immediately rejecting places that looked as if they might present a legitimate threat of werewolf attack. These were dark times.

Now, did I really believe that the light of a full moon would turn an otherwise normal human into a werewolf hell-bent on eating me? Maybe. Yeah, maybe I did. But fear of a werewolf attack was the purest fear I could imagine. It was something so horrible and unnerving that I ran from it for most of my life. I admit it maybe was somewhat unreasonable.

In my early twenties, I forced myself to sit and watch werewolf movie after werewolf movie to try and conquer my bizarre fear. After a while, I began appreciating the aesthetics of these films. The soundtrack, the makeup, the character design, the location scouting, even the intentional and unintentional humor. All of a sudden, my attempts at exposure therapy became an independent study of genre film history. And just like that, not only did I conquer my fear, but it became an enormous source of inspiration.

I had found the best way to conquer fear was by facing it head-on and sometimes even mocking it, with just the right amount of sarcastic nihilism. In the following years after my werewolf marathon, I consumed just about every horror-related piece of media out there. I couldn't get enough. I loved everything from haunted houses and ghost tours to devil-illustrated skateboards and heavy metal–themed pentagram patches on denim vests. The occult had a stranglehold on me and I embraced it.

OPPOSITE:
Nightscape, 2011
Title sequence lettering

NIGHTSCAPE
ROAD WITHOUT END

A
DAVID W. EDWARDS
FILM

AND
SUZANNE OWENS-DUVAL
AS "VESPER"

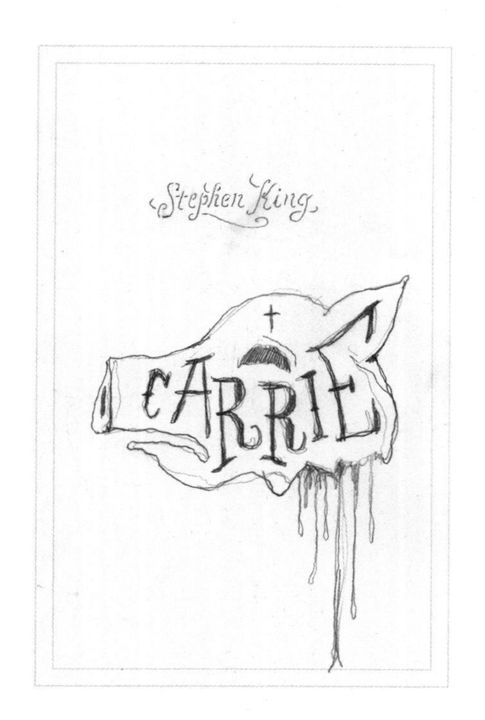

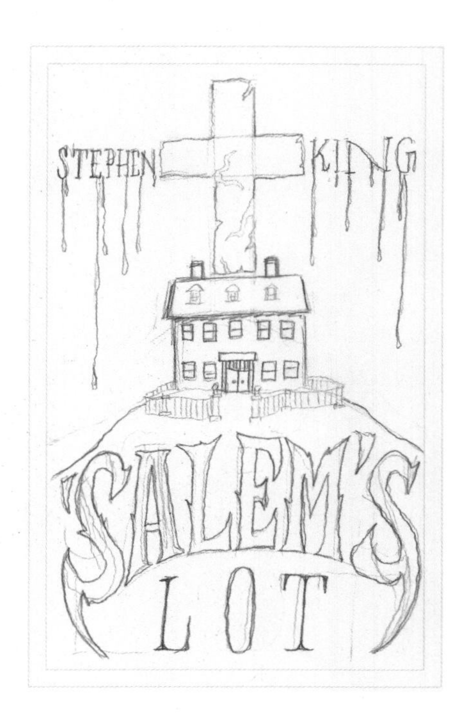

ABOVE:
Sterling Publishing, 2011
Cover concept sketches

OPPOSITE:
Sterling Publishing, 2011
"Three Novels" final cover design

During a late night in the spring of 2011, I was tasked with designing the book-cover art for a special edition bundle of Stephen King's first three novels: *Carrie*, *Salem's Lot*, and *The Shining*.

In order to get in the mindset truly worthy of the books' contents, I sketched concepts in the living room while my wife watched a documentary on serial killers. Later I sat in my home studio, listened to black metal as loud as possible, and found myself researching grotesque images of severed pigs' heads.

After a late night and dozens of sketches, I turned out the lights and went to bed. Needless to say, I was still pretty wired from ingesting hours of extreme horror, so I turned on the television. The film *Jeepers Creepers 2* happened to be on, so I watched it until the end and finally fell asleep during the credits, thus completing a night of total immersion in dread and terror.

The following morning, I awoke to find that not only was I nightmare-free, but I in fact had had the greatest and most refreshing sleep of my entire life. That thought was more unsettling than everything I had seen the night before.

The final artwork ended up looking much less terrifying than I originally intended, but the memory of my complete and utter serenity in the world of horror haunts me to this day.

ABRACADABRA

ABOVE:

Museum of Pop Culture (previously the EMP Museum), 2011

Branding and original concept art

The *Can't Look Away* exhibit, curated by iconic directors Roger Corman, John Landis, and Eli Roth, honored horror's rich history in cinema.

OPPOSITE:

"Abracadabra," 2013

Personal illustration

PROFESSOR NIGHTMARE'S
HOUSE
OF
HORROR'S

PROFESSOR
NIGHTMARE'S
HOUSE
OF
HORRORS

Invisible Threads, 2016

T-shirt illustration for magician-themed apparel brand

Google Cardboard, 2015
"Dreams Incarnated"

These hand-painted Google Cardboard VR headsets were designed and sold to benefit p:ear, a nonprofit that mentors homeless youth in Portland, Oregon.

The
MARVELOUS
AND REMARKABLE
WONDER
-MATIC
All New!

WILL YOU DARE
To
LOOK
BEYOND?

The
MARVELOUS
AND REMARKABLE
WONDER
-MATIC
All New!

Behold
The GREAT ORACLE

MYSTERY

MATIC
All New!

FEAR

PART I: LIFE & DEATH

As soon as you become a grown-up, you need to start making decisions about things. Should I rent this apartment even though it might be beyond my means? Am I ready to become a father? Is it appropriate to wear basketball shorts in public anymore? Some choices are easy and some are pretty tough, but it's all on you.

It was only a matter of time before the anxiety of all this crept into my life and started wreaking havoc. Life gets difficult at some point for everyone; you can't get away with playing LEGO with your little brother in your parents' basement forever. It happens sooner than later for some, but we all end up dealing with it. Hell, I woke up in a panicked state this morning for absolutely no discernable reason. I honestly can't articulate what I'm worried about, but I know it's something, and it's not making me happy. (And it's definitely not making my wife happy either, because now she has to deal with my moody ass.) Maybe there's some old, horrific fear still bouncing around in the back of my head without me even realizing.

I can easily pinpoint key moments in my life that have been absolutely terrifying. Like, so terrifying you suddenly need to buy a new pair of pants. But here's the thing: I'm still here and I'm talking about it, so clearly it wasn't that bad.

Daniel Trocchio is a tattoo artist working in Brooklyn whose work I first saw over a decade ago. This guy has some absolutely killer stuff. There's this one piece I discovered during a gallery show he was featured in that I became absolutely obsessed with. It was this super dark reaper image, and beneath it, Trocchio had lettered: "Nine-tenths of your life I'll strangle from you, the last tenth will make you strong." At the time, I was broke as hell, so there was no way I could afford to buy a print. The best I could do to remember the piece was sneakily shoot a crappy, pixelated photo of it with my flip-phone camera.

A few years later I was getting tattooed at a shop in Greenpoint, Brooklyn, called Three Kings when I happened to find out Trocchio worked there. I immediately ran downstairs to his station, asked him about the piece, and set up an appointment, and I got it permanently etched into my skin as soon as he was available. Much better than a flip-phone jpeg. Never has anything so perfectly fit the mantra I long ago learned to live by.

On many occasions, I've sat down with business owners struggling to make decisions over the design treatment of their brand. In typical Jon Contino overly dramatic fashion, I like to say: "We're all going to die, so let's do something awesome." I mean, I have no intent on harming the client, but at some point, Father Time is going to do his job and take us all out. I've seen what it looks like to be on the brink of death, and there's no amount of copy revisions or new sketches that will change that. We all have a desire to build something, and I've made it my mission to help people explore that.

If you've ever decided to create, you know the work comes from deep down inside. It's something you feel needs to be introduced to the universe for some reason. Maybe it's the greatest thing ever or maybe it's total garbage—but the minute we second-guess our ideas is the instant our gift of creativity dies. The moment we throw away hesitation and face our fears of failure and uncertainty, the real-life magic happens—innovation happens.

The greatest ideas never come from a person in a comfortable emotional state. They come from torment and frustration and complete and total anxiety. You have to be completely irrational to summon the creativity you were born with.

Sometimes it's hard to talk about this kind of thing because art and design aren't life or death. There are so many atrocities happening every second in every corner of the world that making a creative decision feels pretty low on the ladder of global significance. And yet, for those of us lucky enough to be able to live safely and work toward making something, we still have fears every single day. We still have to face bad news or cope with shitty luck and have reasons we don't want to get out of bed in the morning. But if you can embrace fear and welcome the hard decisions that come with it, then it can become the catalyst to greatness.

ROUGH SEAS AHEAD
HURLEY

RAISING HELL CHASING SWELL
DePALMA CC

BEYOND THE WATCH

TIME AIN'T WAITING ON YOU

SEE YOU IN HELL

FIND YOURSELF

C&M MFG. '13
BORN TO
RAISE HELL

2017
"YOUR MOVE"

FOREVER
INPRNT

KEEP 'EM
COMIN'!

THIS SPREAD & PREVIOUS:
Various reapers, 2010–2017

I've always loved the tangible manifestation of death as a character. There are so many statements you can make with the embodiment of certain doom. It can be damning or inspirational. But mostly it's just really cool.

JC
197

PART II: FRUS-FUCKIN-STRATION

We have a saying in my family: "Continos don't have bad luck, we have hard luck." It's become something of an inside joke at this point, but essentially it means that nothing comes easy and anything worth having is worth fighting for. Nothing is just going to happen and make life great, that's not the way the world works. At least, not for most people. You're not always going to be acknowledged for doing something special, you won't always be celebrated for succeeding, and you certainly won't be paid what you deserve, if you're even paid at all. Hell, sometimes you're lucky if you just break even. But that's what you get with hard luck. You get a chance, and that's all you really need.

Sometimes hard luck gets so bad you start praying for life to turn around and throw you a bone. Like, when is the universe gonna cut you some slack for two goddamn minutes already. Frustration can build slowly. Little things peck away at you until you can't quite handle it anymore. You'll get so worked up that the idea of relief seems impossible, but if you were to step outside yourself for two seconds, you'd realize none of these things are really major issues. It's just the consistency that wears you down. And man, can it wear you down.

I've been there more times than I'd like to count. In 2009, my best friend (and former partner in my old design studio Onetwentysix) Matt Gorton and I started CXXVI Clothing Company on a budget of zero dollars. We printed shirts using leftovers from our clients, built a web store out of what seemed like duct tape and bubble gum, shot the lookbook in an afternoon on the docks behind our studio, and eventually turned eight simple T-shirts into a legitimate full-time business with employees in less than a year's time. We turned nothing into something, and we were excited to finally see progress after suffering through the knockdown blow of the Great Recession.

As our business grew, we needed to take on investment partners to help finance production. All was well for a few years until one major retail chain declared bankruptcy and liquidated well over a hundred thousand dollars of our merchandise without having paid a single cent for it. It left Matt and me on the hook for the entire production cost without having any actual cash to back it up. And then to top it off, Hurricane Sandy came charging in and wiped out our entire studio, remaining inventory, and most of what we had left of the brand. After we lost nearly everything, our trade-show booths were so barren they looked like a five-year-old's lemonade stand. We had massive bills and no way to pay them. It wasn't exactly the way we'd planned on making it big. Our stress levels were immeasurable, the strain on our friendship was pushing it to the breaking point, and there didn't seem to be any way out.

Oh, and how could I forget this beautiful little detail: On the day that I buried my grandmother, one of the closest people in my life, I was getting threatening calls from collections agencies while still standing at her grave. But don't worry, it gets worse. As Matt and I attempted to pay back this unexpected debt over the next year or so, my grandfather passed away. And you guessed it: threatening calls at the cemetery yet again. Was I being watched? Was there some van marked FLORIST with a giant radio antenna on top just waiting to get me at my weakest moment? I was beginning to feel like there was a giant conspiracy to see how much torture my life could take until I did something crazy. I have never considered myself a bad person. I never did drugs or smoked or even drank alcohol. I have always tried to help whomever I could in any situation and to be compassionate toward anyone, even if they didn't deserve it. And yet here I stood, my company obliterated, my best friend estranged, my beloved grandparents gone, and phone calls threatening lawsuits like I was some sort of delinquent dirtbag looking to scam people. This is not what I expected from starting a simple T-shirt company. They don't teach you this shit in school.

To say I was frustrated is a bit of an understatement. No one had taught me about the pitfalls of starting a business and certainly no one had told me about the worst-case scenario, but there I was. Staring into the abyss. Wondering what was next. Where could I go? What could I do? Something needed to change, and I didn't know when or if I'd ever get the opportunity to give it another shot.

Things turned around after that. Matt and I went our separate ways for a bit and freelanced nonstop until we were both able to collectively pay back the debt. We dealt with the worst and realized we were still alive and kicking, and the stress finally started to disappear. At last, we could be friends again. I made sure to take better precautions after all this, but frustration will always come back around again at some point. There will always be an endless number of roadblocks keeping the world from being permanently happy. Some people have it harder than others, but the way you respond is what determines your actual success. When all is said and done, your actions will speak louder than any bump in the road ever could.

CATCH ME
IF YOU CAN

In God We Must, 2017

Various illustrations for the clothing, jewelry, and lifestyle brand

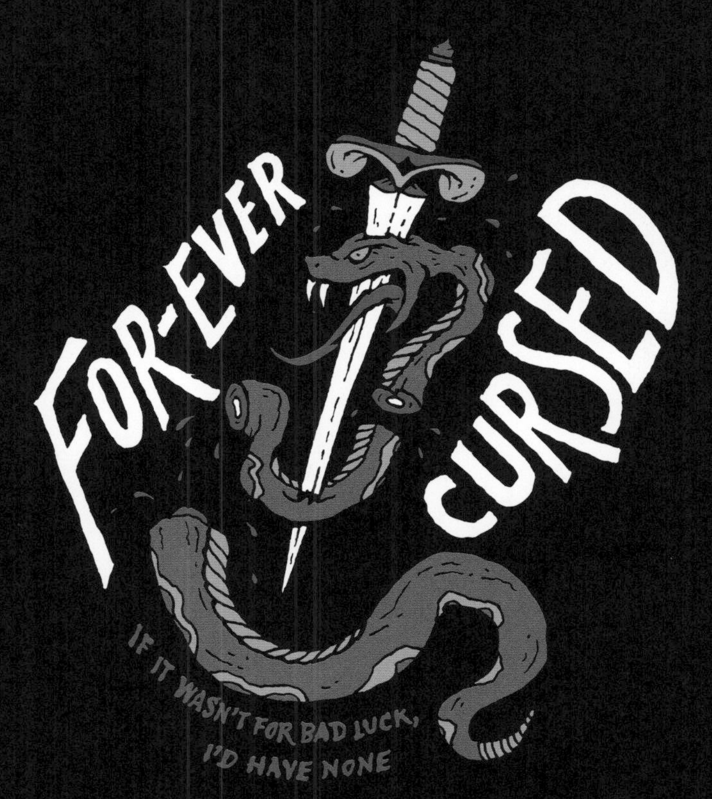

TOP:
Nike, 2014
Various illustrations

ABOVE FROM LEFT:
In God We Must, 2017, "It's O.K." clothing graphic;
Secret Artist Society, 2012, "For-Ever Cursed" T-shirt graphic

J. Contino for Stock Mfg.

"The Phantom Collection"
A Collaboration b'tween
Jon Contino & Stock Mfg.
New York and Chicago
Made in the U.S.A.

Behold, the Phantom
Shrouded in Mystery

DON'T TURN YOUR BACK
ON THE PHANTOM

Stock Mfg., 2014

"The Phantom Collection"

The goal of this project was to create a beautifully minimal menswear collection with a ton of hidden gems—fun illustrated details in areas most people wouldn't normally see, hence the name of the collection. Also, the slithering snake wearing an executioner's hood might be my favorite thing I've ever designed.

ROME
SDS
RESTLESS & HUNGRY
"CROSSROCKET"
154
HIGHEST QUALITY
Jon Contino
NEW YORK, N.Y.
For
ROME SDS

ROME
SDS

"CROSSROCKET"

156

HIGHEST QUALITY

NO REGRETS

Jon Contino
NEW YORK, N.Y.
For
ROME SDS

Rome SDS, 2013

These hand-engraved found weapons were photographed to be used as the primary images on the 2015 "Crossrocket" snowboard series.

ROME SDS
CRØSSRØCKET
RO
ME
SNOWBOARD
DESIGN
SYNDICATE
162
CRØSSRØCKET

Rome SDS, 2012–2016

Seasonal snowboards and artwork for the "Crossrocket" series

2–2016

hirt illustrations

DRINK WITH HONOR
DIE WITH RESPECT
HANOI, VIET NAM
Rocurk

Toyota, 2017

"Hotel Tacoma" branding system

A metallic, fire-breathing bunny totem and the legend of the Pacific Northwest himself, Sasquatch, both served as inspiration for Toyota's exclusive woodland getaway adventure to promote the Tacoma truck. These examples are small pieces of a larger system of branded icons, merchandise, and signage.

The "Sasquatch peace head" is one of my favorite marks I've ever designed. The Sasquatch head represents the location of the event, the skullface represents danger, the hand giving "bunny ears" represents fun, but there's still a friendly, "peaceful" nature of all involved. I crammed a lot into that one.

BELL

VXCC
BRONX, N.Y.
YOUR LUNGS ARE BURNING.
YOUR LEGS ARE SHREDDED.
AND THIS IS JUST THE BEGINNING.
WE ARE A DIFFERENT BREED.
DON'T BE AFRAID.
LET YOUR ANIMAL INSTINCTS
KICK IN AS YOU DEVOUR THE PACK.
THIS IS MILES OF AGONY VS ECSTASY
INJURIES BE DAMNED.
THE THRILL OF THE HUNT DRIVES
YOU TO SLAY YOUR OPPONENT.
PAIN IS TEMPORARY,
VICTORY IS ETERNAL.
YOU CAN TASTE IT.

EARN NYC
RUN HUNGRY
20 12
TASTE VICTORY
XC
TORTOISE AND HARE
RUNNED OVER
7
2

Nike, 2012

"VCXC" identity design for a race and pop-up shop at Van Cortlandt Park in the Bronx

The Van Cortlandt Park trail is known as one of the toughest, most treacherous cross-country running courses in the nation. Branding a race held on this hardcore trail was a blast, but painting the accompanying mural was a humbling experience (a slap in the face, really). I showed up early on setup day so that I'd have time to finesse the finer details of the design, but I soon realized a light projector in the middle of a hot, bright August afternoon would not display my design clearly enough on the wall. I was forced to wait until dusk settled in around 8 P.M. to start painting as quickly as I could, and I was still working well past 3 A.M.

LEAD FROM THE FRONT

DON'T STOP
DON'T YIELD

ABCDEFGHIJKLM
NOPQRSTUVWXYZ

PASS AT YOUR OWN PERIL

DON'T STOP
DON'T YIELD

Put it on the Line

Nike, 2013
"We Run" identity design for international racing series and retail locations

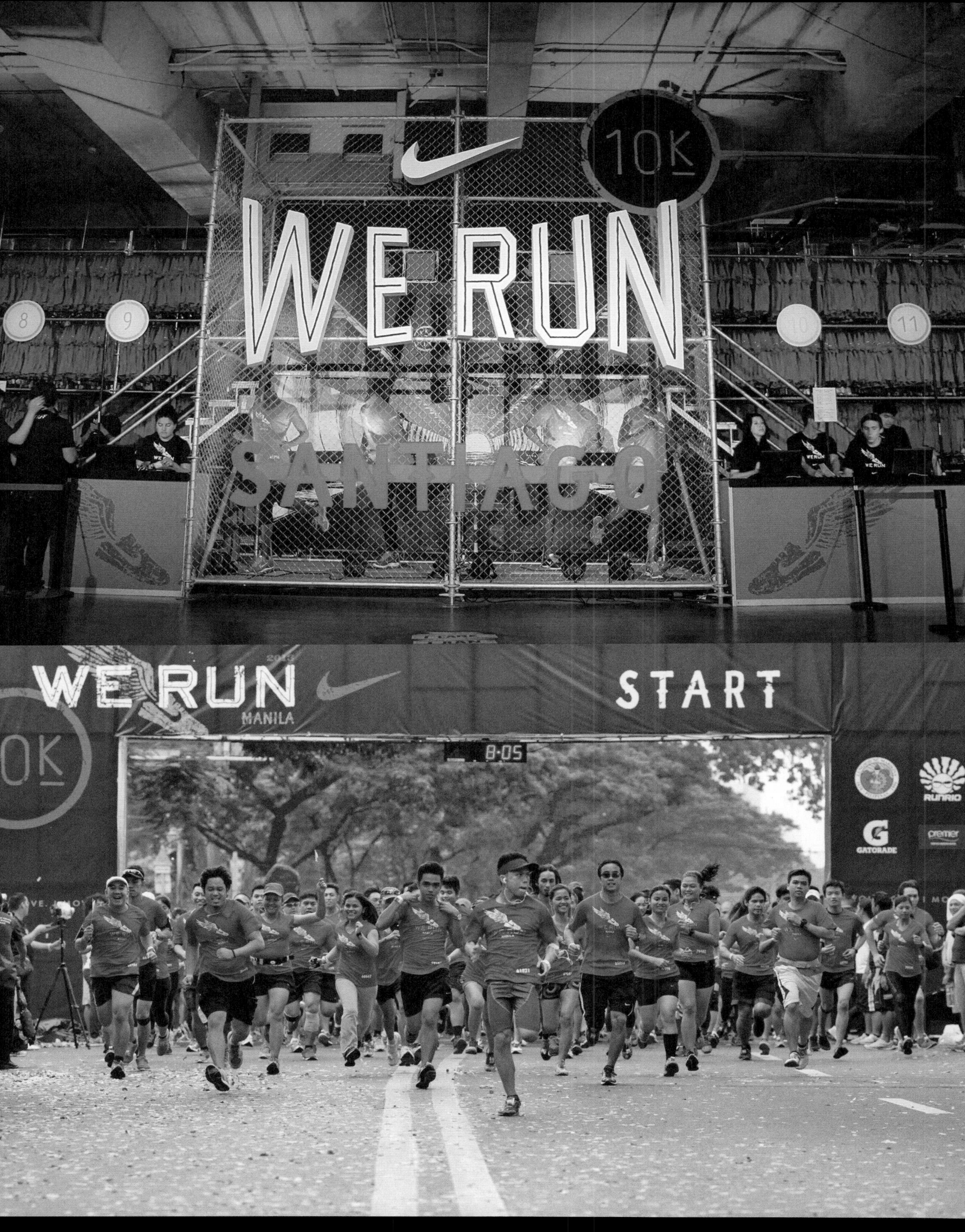
10K
WE RUN
SANTIAGO
WE RUN
MANILA
START
8:05
GATORADE
RUNRIO

FERDINAND
DISCOVER THE TRUTH BEHIND THE BULL
DECEMBER 15

20th Century Fox, 2016

Ferdinand

Promotional posters to announce the release of the animated film *Ferdinand*, designed in various styles to support the film's central theme of "uniqueness"

Vices

I DON'T SMOKE,
I DON'T DRINK, and
I DON'T DO DRUGS.

I've never done any of these things. I'm pretty sure it has to do with the fact that I'm a total control freak, and anything that could possibly break me out of my shell for even a minute is my mortal enemy. That being said, for something so antithetical to my most basic instincts, the culture of these vices sure has a history of some really cool looking stuff. No argument there.

Leather-clad flasks, Vietnam-era Zippo lighters, screen-printed beer koozies, engraved cigarette cases . . . The list goes on and on. It's a creative gold mine. The history of beer labels alone is enough to send someone down a very specific career path. There's something about appealing to adults who are attempting to enjoy life that brings out the best in design. Sure, these products are not associated with the healthiest practices by any means, but aesthetically speaking, there's a lot of really good shit out there. You can't hide from the purpose of these products. They are what they are and they do what they do. That's it. So taking the opportunity to design them can be pretty liberating, especially for a wiseass adult.

For example, when I mark up a Zippo lighter, I know it's not intended for kids, so there's no reason to censor the concept behind the design. Most likely it's going to be in the possession of another wiseass adult and most likely will be mocked or praised by secondary wiseasses in the vicinity of said original wiseass. The math is all there. I mean, let's be honest here, booze and cigarettes are meant to be an escape from the typical constructs of everyday life, so why not have some fun with them?

Designing around a vice is the grown-up version of drawing raunchy shit in a high school bathroom or carving something obnoxious into your desk in chemistry class. It's elevated and degenerate all within the same breath. It's the perfect time to be childish and free-swinging with stuff that you probably shouldn't be so serious about in the first place.

OPPOSITE:
Hand-engraved lighter, 2009

GOD
DAMN
THEM
ALL

The Hidden Sea

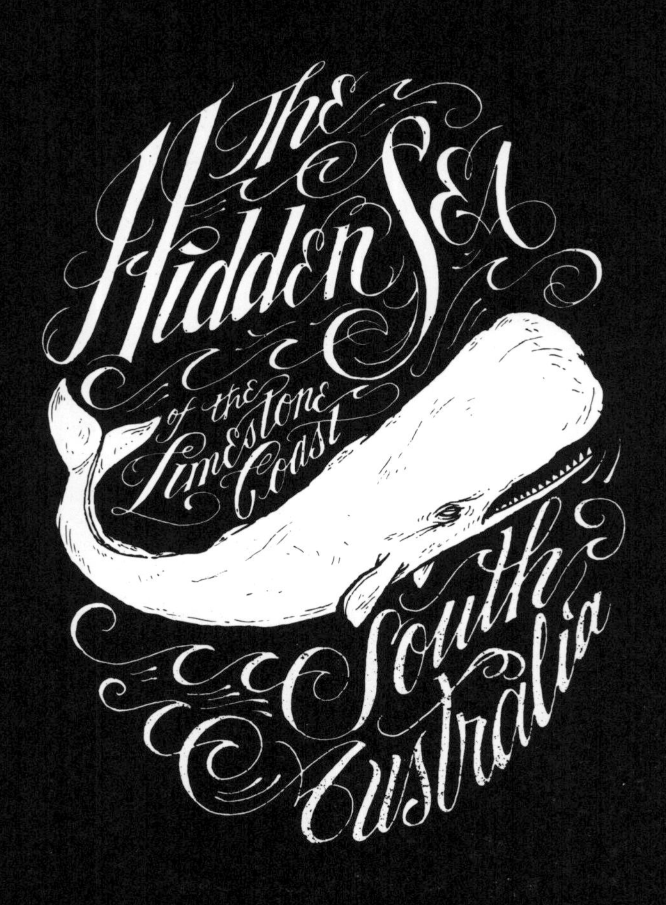

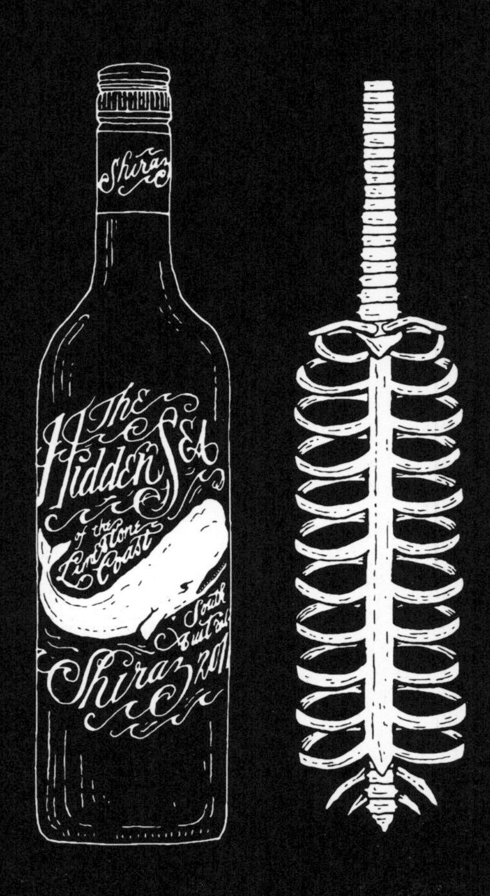

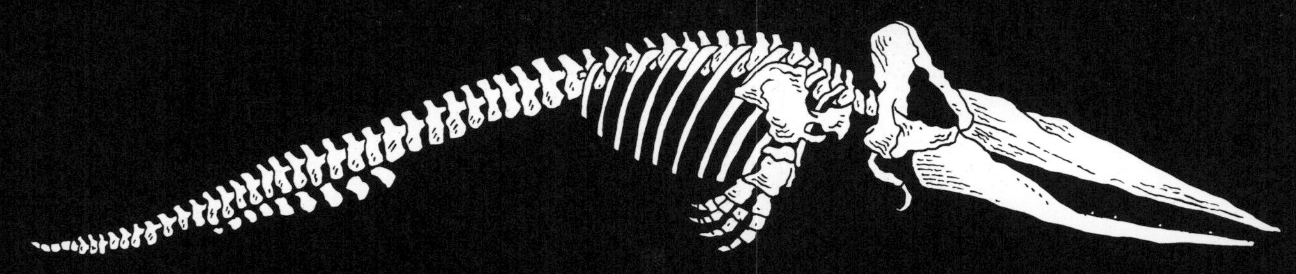

The Hidden Sea, 2011–2017
Identity, package design, and direction for South Australian–based wine company

ROME SDS

OR YOU'RE A

ROME SDS

ROME SDS

LOOK TO THE

AND SIP

OR A STORM TO ROLL

PASS THE TIME

SINCE 2001

Rome SDS, 2012

"Crossrocket" snowboard series

ABOVE:
Texas Monthly, 2013, 2015
Magazine cover lettering using food and condiments as the medium

OPPOSITE:
21st Amendment, 2011, 2012
"Hop Crisis" and "Marooned on Hog Island" beer packaging

HOP CRISIS
Imperial IPA
THE HOP SYNDICATE IS HOARDING HOPS IN A REMOTE WAREHOUSE. THIS IS NOT COOL.
WE HAVE TO DO SOMETHING.
WE HAVE TO BREAK OUT OF ALCATRAZ. AND FAST.
NO ONE HAS EVER ESCAPED FROM ALCATRAZ! ...EXCEPT IN THE MOVIES.
GOOD POINT SULLY.
FOUR
21ST-AMENDMENT.COM
21A
ALE AGED ON OAK SPIRALS
DURING THE HOP CRISIS, SOME BREWERS WERE FORCED TO SKIMP ON HOPS, DEPRIVING THE PEOPLE OF THEIR RIGHT TO HOPPY, AROMATIC BEER.

WITH THE HELP OF A COUPLE OF DUCATS OF LEAD SHOT, THESE BEER MUTINEERS AND OYSTER MERCENARIES WERE SOON STRADDLING A ROARING FIRE AND FEASTING ON ROAST PIG, FRESHLY SHUCKED OYSTERS, AND GOBLETS OF FINE ALE. THEY COULD THINK OF WORSE FATES THAN BEING...
Marooned on Hog Island
STOUT BREWED WITH HOG ISLAND SWEETWATER OYSTER SHELLS
21A
HOG ISLAND OYSTER
21ST-AMENDMENT.COM

TROUBARDOUR

TOP:
Beery Christmas, 2016
Craft brewery advent calendar

ABOVE:
Troubardour, 2017
Identity design for a mobile bar
and entertainment service

Miller High Life, 2013

Harley Davidson artist series

Pedal Haus Brewery, 2015

Identity and environmental branding

STILL
DEATH

DEATH

Hand-engraved lighters, 2010–2017

I don't remember exactly when I picked up a Dremel engraver, sometime around 2007 maybe. The first thing I marked up was a metal wallet my wife bought me. After that, engraving became a way to "tattoo" any hard surface I could get my hands on. During the Project NY menswear trade show in 2010, I had the bright idea of customizing lighters as a way of promoting CXXVI and getting press to our booth so people would buy our clothes. It definitely grabbed attention, and offering custom-engraved lighters became a staple of my product work for years to come.

VI
Lucky
LIBERTY OR DEATH
ROTTEN EYES
II
DEEP IN THE HEART
2017
L.I.
NO GUTS NO GLORY!
2016
BUCK UP
V
LIVE FAST DIE YOUNG
III

2011
VOL. I

2011
VOL. II

2012
VOL. I

2012
VOL. II

2014 VOL. I

2014 VOL. II

2015 VOL. I

2015 VOL. II

ACKNOWLEDGMENTS

My most sincere thanks to John Gall and the entire team at Abrams Books for getting this project in motion and holding my hand the entire way through. This has been a dream come true, and I can't express my feelings of appreciation enough. Thank you to my incredible wife, Erin, for everything, but more specifically for helping me with each and every detail that lives on these pages. You're the greatest thing to ever happen to me, and I continue to reap the benefits of being under the same roof with you every day. Thank you to my amazing daughter, Fiona, for going through all of this work with me and giving me brutally honest and extremely thoughtful commentary, over and over again. I can't wait until your first book comes out. Thank you to my parents, Vito and Christine, for all you've done, but especially for giving me a loving household to grow up in free of judgment. Your belief in me and wise words shaped the man I am today, and I'm thankful to be able to keep learning from you even to this day. Thank you to my brothers, Nick and Chris, for always keeping me on my toes while still being the best teammates in life anyone could ask for. Thank you to all my family and friends who have supported me over the years, no matter how crazy I may have seemed. Thank you to Matt Gorton for being a great business partner and an even better friend. The journey we've been on together has been wild. Thank you to Todd Radom for being an inspiring mentor and someone I am proud to call a friend. Thank you to Brent Bates for helping me organize all this stuff into something that makes sense. Thank you to Matt Fox and Zombie Apocalypse for allowing me to use an excerpt from "March On to Victory." And of course, thank you to all of my clients and collaborators, past, present, and future.

Without all of you, absolutely none of this would be possible!

CREDITS

Page 41: Andrew Livingston
Page 43: Scott Goodman
Pages 47, 50-51, 53: Matt Gorton
Page 63: Hamilton Wood Type & Printing Museum
Page 64: Home of the Brave
Page 73: Scott Delbango
Page 91: Marissa McClain
Page 100: Erik Attkisson
Page 102: Erin Sfarra
Page 107: Mathew Zucker
Page 128: Erin Contino
Pages 134-137: Journal Standard Furniture
Pages 152-153: Proyecto Ensamble
Page 176: Album cover painting by Tim Lehi
Page 177: Dan Rawe
Page 178: The Museum of Pop Culture
Page 188: Instrument
Page 205: Stock Mfg.
Pages 206-207: Michael Paddock
Page 213: Saatchi LA
Pages 214, 217: Nike
Page 225: Dean Schmideg
Page 229: TBD Agency
Page 230: Interdrinks
Page 230: Mino Yaki Pottery
Page 232: Blair Bunting

HOCUS-POCUS
MOTHERFUCKER

"SEE YA!"

THOSE WHO FEAR J
ONLY THEMS
EXISTENCE • BUT
COMES • THOSE W
BE THE ONES WHO
WEAPON • SO WE
ON TO VICTORY • GE
MARCH ON TO VIC
FEET BLEED • THE